A Faculty Theory of Knowledge

A Faculty Theory of Knowledge

THE AIM AND SCOPE OF HUME'S FIRST *Enquiry*

George Stern

Lewisburg
BUCKNELL UNIVERSITY PRESS

Associated University Presses, Inc.
Cranbury, New Jersey 08512

ISBN: 0-8387-7821-6
Printed in the United States of America

To my wife, Dvora

Contents

Contents

A Faculty Theory of Knowledge

"[The] assumption that the exegesis of Hume was in effect finished needs to be challenged."

T. E. Jessop, in
"Some Misunderstandings of Hume," 1952

1
Introduction

Hume and His Predecessors

This book is primarily concerned with a critical presentation of a theory of knowledge unique to the eighteenth-
century Scottish philosopher David Hume. Although parts
of this theory are contained in Hume's other works, the
complete system can be found only in his *Enquiry concerning the Human Understanding*,[1] usually known as
the first *Enquiry*, which appeared in its initial edition in
1748.

The scientific and philosophical atmosphere of the late
seventeenth and most of the eighteenth century was dominated by Isaac Newton's works. Their importance derives
only partly from the fact that they capped and superseded

1. D. Hume, *Enquiries concerning the Human Understanding and concerning the Principles of Morals*, reprinted from the posthumous edition
of 1777 and edited with introduction, comparative tables of contents,
and analytic index by L. A. Selby-Bigge, 2nd ed. (Oxford: Oxford University Press, 1902).

the work of Newton's predecessors in astronomy mathematics and physics. Of equal importance is the fact that they inaugurated a remarkable era of intensive, though mainly theoretical, investigations into these same sciences the practical fruits of which were born a hundred years later in the industrial revolution.

The scientific endeavors of the Newtonian period stimulated, and were stimulated by, a resurgence of philosophical activity. While much of this activity still centered on controversies generated in the post-Renaissance era, there was also, not surprisingly for an age of rapid expansion in many fields of knowledge, a marked renewal of interest in questions concerned with the methods and validity of knowledge. Here too Newton exerted a direct influence through his "Rules of Reasoning in Philosophy" (from the *Philosophiae Naturalis Principia Mathematica*, 1687), which served as a point of departure for subsequent empiricist systems.

Late seventeenth- and eighteenth-century epistemological doctrines, whether Newtonian or non-Newtonian in orientation, were characterized by two leading principles: that perfect or indubitable knowledge is attainable in at least some field or fields of enquiry, and that basically all knowledge is of a kind. For convenience, we might refer to the first of these principles as the principle of epistemological confidence, and to the second as the principle of methodological simplicity. Taken together they lead to the view that, once the philosopher has uncovered a method of acquiring perfect knowledge in one field, the same method can then be extended to all other fields that are subject to intellectual investigation. Consequently, the goal of certainty in all departments of knowledge was held to be theoretically attainable, and epistemologists concentrated on the task of finding the right means to the attainment of this goal.

There were considerable differences in the methods advocated by various philosophers of the period. These ranged from the deductivist theories of Cartesians and the intuitionist theories of Cambridge Platonists to the empiricism of Locke and to Malebranche's theory that knowledge was implanted in the human mind by God. But for all their tactical differences on the right method, philosophers were generally agreed on the strategic concept that there was one such primary method leading to knowledge in all fields of intellectual endeavor. One apparent exception to this agreement was the Theists' adherence to the dichotomy of reason and revelation as two distinct if complementary sources of knowledge. But this dichotomy is also reducible to methodological simplicity by virtue of the Theists' claim that the truth of revelation can be rationally demonstrated.

Hume's writings constitute a genuine and radical dissent from the principle of methodological simplicity. In his first work, the *Treatise of Human Nature* (1739-40),[2] he discredits the principle by making explicit the absurd consequences which arise when certain rational methods which do provide good grounds for epistemological confidence in one cognitive field are applied to other fields. In the first *Enquiry* he goes on to construct an epistemological system based on the opposing principle of methodological complexity. This is what he has called a "mental geography" or, in modern terms, a faculty theory of knowledge. Its leading feature is the denial of the extensibility of any method that assures us of knowledge in one cogni-

2. D. Hume, *A Treatise of Human Nature* (London: J. M. Dent & Sons, 1911).

tive field to all, or even to any one of, the others. Hume argues that the "human understanding" is endowed with a variety of faculties, and that each of these is uniquely fitted for the investigation of one and only one class of cognitive object. It is the critical presentation of this faculty theory of knowledge that is the main concern of the present work.

The Exegesis of Hume

Although Hume's work has been subjected to over two centuries of analysis and criticism, the critics are even now hopelessly divided on the correct interpretation of his individual doctrines and on the implications of his philosophy taken as a whole. One point of disagreement concerns the critics' evaluation of Hume's attitude to the principle of epistemological confidence. Most consider his philosophy to be consistent with one form or another of scepticism; others deny that his conclusions are sceptical at all.[3] Again, there are discrepant views on whether it was Hume's intention in the *Treatise* and in the first *Enquiry* to establish an epistemology in its own right[4] or whether this epistemological system, whatever it might

3. Even allowing for differences in the definition of the term, there is a wide divergence of views on this question. R. E. Hobart argues the minority opinion in "Hume without Scepticism", *Mind*, 39 (1939). Among those who attribute an extreme form of scepticism to Hume are T. Reid, *Essays on the Intellectual Powers of Man*, ed. A. D. Woozley (London: Macmillan, 1941), p. 133; R. M. Chisholm, *Perceiving: A Philosophical Study* (Ithaca, N. Y.: Cornell University Press, 1957), chapter 4; H. A. Prichard, *Knowledge and Perception* (Oxford: Oxford University Press, 1950), pp. 174 ff. Intermediate positions are taken by J. A. Passmore, *Hume's Intentions* (Cambridge: Cambridge University Press, 1952), chapter 7; R. W. Church, *Hume's Theory of the Understanding* (London: George Allen and Unwin, 1935), Introduction; A. Flew, *Hume's Philosophy of Belief* (London: Routledge and Kegan Paul, 1961), chapter 10.
4. See C. Maund, *Hume's Theory of Knowledge* (London: Macmillan, 1937), chapter 2.

be, served as a digressive preliminary to his ethical[5] or perhaps his religious[6] theories. Hume has been regarded as a subjectivist and an objectivist,[7] an atheist and a "reverent agnostic",[8] a phenomenalist,[9] a positivist,[10] a neutral monist,[11] and a solipsist.[12] The only point on which there does appear to be agreement is that his writings are paradigms of style and clarity!

One explanation that has been offered to account for some of the confusion over the correct interpretation of Hume is this:

It is a common practice of philosophers who have either not understood, or not responded sympathetically, to Hume's views, to use what to me, are at least misleading presentations, if not complete travesties of them, to illuminate by contrast either their own opinions, or those of philosophers whom they appreciate.[13]

I believe that the confusion is attributable to several other reasons besides these enumerated by Maund. One of these is that the usual method of expounding Hume's

5. This was first seriously proposed by N. K. Smith, *The Philosophy of David Hume* (London: Macmillan, 1964), chapter 1. See also T. E. Jessop, "Some Misunderstandings of Hume", *Revue Internationale de Philosophie*, 6 (1952) ; J. A. Passmore, chapter 1; and A. H. Basson, *David Hume* (Harmondsworth: Penguin Books, 1958).
6. This is the contention of C. W. Hendel, *Studies in the Philosophy of David Hume* (Princeton: Princeton University Press, 1925), chapter 1.
7. Again allowing for various definitions of the terms involved, Hume is generally held to be the former. But for a contrary view, see T. E. Jessop, p. 167.
8. *Ibid.* p. 157.
9. D. M. Armstrong, *Perception and the Physical World* (London: Routledge and Kegan Paul, 1961), chapter 4; and W. S. Haymond, "Hume's Phenomenalism," *The Modern Schoolman*, 41 (1963–64).
10. See, for example, Passmore, chapter 4.
11. H. H. Price groups Hume with Mach and Russell under this head in *Hume's Theory of the External World* (Oxford: Oxford University Press, 1940), p. 105.
12. C. Hartshorne, "Hume's Metaphysics and Its Present-Day Influence," *The New Scholasticism*, 25 (1961) ; and A. Flew, pp. 246 f.
13. C. Maund, "On the Nature and Significance of Hume's Scepticism," *Revue Internationale de Philosophie*, 6 (1952) : p. 182.

philosophy has been to consider one or another of his doctrines in isolation: his theory of causality, his critique of induction, his analysis of the notion of the self, his refutation of the argument from design, and so forth. The conclusions of these doctrines, when taken individually, lend themselves to monist, phenomenalist, subjectivist, sceptical, and similar interpretations; and these interpretations have been extended to Hume's philosophy as a whole.

The preoccupation with Hume's individual doctrines is, in turn, largely due to critical neglect of the first *Enquiry*. When Hume's epistemology is under consideration, it is the *Treatise* and not the *Enquiry* that critics consult as their primary source. Yet the *Enquiry* is the only work in which Hume draws together the various strands of doctrine regarding religion, ethics, perception, and inductive and deductive reasoning—the elements of his mental geography. In each of his other works, the *Treatise* included, only a part of this central thesis is utilised though the whole is assumed. The critics, however, do not generally recognize the claim that Hume's epistemology is a faculty theory of knowledge, nor do they recognize the claim that his epistemology is contained *in toto* in the *Enquiry*.[14]

Consequently, before we can examine Hume's epistemology in detail, it is necessary first to evaluate the current theories regarding the relative importance of the

---

14. In *Hume's Philosophy of Belief*, a work devoted to an analysis of the *Enquiry*, Flew acknowledges that the mental geography is central to Hume's epistemology. After only cursory consideration, however, Flew concludes that this is an unworkable concept, suggests substituting "logical mapwork" for Hume's notion, and virtually ignores both concepts after his first chapter. As the title of his book suggests, Flew sees the *Enquiry* as embodying not a mental geography but rather a "philosophy of belief."

Treatise and the *Enquiry* to an understanding of his philosophy, and to establish the main lines of his epistemology. These preliminary questions are investigated in the next two chapters.

Treatise and the *Enquiry* to an understanding of his

2

The *Treatise* and the *Enquiry*

The Republication Theory

It is a curious feature of Hume's philosophical writings
that each of the themes dealt with in the three Books
of his first work, *The Treatise of Human Nature* (1739),
was dealt with again in a subsequent work. The theme
of Book I, *Of the Understanding,* appeared in a new guise
in the *Enquiry concerning the Human Understanding*
in 1748; that of Book II, *Of the Passions,* reappeared
under the same title as the second of his *Four Dissertations*
in 1757; and that of Book III, *Of Morals,* reemerged in
the *Enquiry concerning the Principles of Morals* in 1751.

Considerable critical attention has been directed at the
question of the relative importance of each work in these
pairs for the understanding of Hume's philosophy in the

relevant field, and to the question of what relationship the members of each pair bear to each other. The way in which these questions are answered in relation to the first pair, Book I of *The Treatise of Human Nature* and *The Enquiry concerning the Human Understanding,* makes a considerable difference to the interpretation of Hume's epistemology. But the converse also holds true: preconceptions concerning the interpretation of Hume's epistemology seem to affect the way in which the questions are answered.

On the question of relative importance, the critics have been in general agreement over the last two centuries that *Treatise I* is a more important source for the understanding of Hume's epistemology than is the first *Enquiry.* On the other question, that of the relationship between these two works, critical opinion seems to be equally divided between two theories.

The first of these may be called the republication theory. The fullest version of it is to be found in the comparison of the *Treatise* and the *Enquiry* undertaken by Vinding Kruse.[1] That writer concludes that the difference between the two works is "merely of a formal nature": that is, discounting a few omissions from the *Treatise* and a few additions to the *Enquiry,* the latter work is substantially a republication in varied form of the substance of the former. In favor of this thesis Kruse adduces what he calls external and internal evidence. The former is elicited by citing Hume to the effect that he himself regarded the two works as being substantially the same, and by presenting a plausible motivation for Hume in recasting the doctrines of the *Treatise.* The in-

---

1. V. Kruse, *Hume's Philosophy in His Principal Work: A Treatise of Human Nature and in His Essays.* Trans. P. T. Federspiel (London: Oxford University Press, 1939) .

ternal evidence consists of a close comparison of the contents of the two works. The whole of this evidence deserves some investigation since it—or at least major elements of it—will be found to form the argument of a wide range of critics who subscribe to the republication theory.[2]

The key passages taken as indicative of Hume's attitude to the question are extracted from one of his letters and from his "Advertisement" to the *Enquiry:*

> "I believe the philosophical Essays contain every thing of Consequence relating to the Understanding which you woud meet with in the Treatise; & I give you my Advice against reading the latter. By shortening & simplifying the Questions, I really render them much more complete. *Addo dum minuo.* The philosophical Principles are the same in both . . ."[3]
> "Most of the Principles, and reasonings, contained in this volume, were published in a work in three volumes, called *A Treatise of Human Nature* . . ."[4]

These passages are manifestly open to the interpretation suggested by the republication theory. However, they are also open to the interpretation that, while the assumptions underlying both works are the same, they neverthe-

---

2. T. Reid, *Essays on the Intellectual Powers of Man*, ed. A. D. Woozley (London: Macmillan, 1941) , p. 130; L. A. Selby-Bigge in his introduction to D. Hume, *Enquiries concerning the Human Understanding and concerning the Principles of Morals*, 2nd ed. (Oxford: Oxford University Press, 1902) ; A. H. Basson, *David Hume* (Harmondsworth: Penguin Books, 1958) , pp. 15 f.; T. E. Jessop, "Some Misunderstandings of Hume," *Revue Internationale de Philosophie* 6 (1952) : 163; C. Maund, *Hume's Theory of Knowledge* (London: Macmillan, 1937) , pp. 28 ff.; B. M. Laing, *David Hume* (London: Ernest Benn, 1932) , p. 31; D. G. C. MacNabb, "David Hume," *The Encyclopedia of Philosophy*, 4, ed. Paul Edwards (New York: Macmillan and Free Press, 1967) : 74f.; and N. K. Smith in his edition of Hume's *Dialogues concerning Natural Religion*, 2nd ed. with supplement (Edinburgh: Nelson, 1947) , p. 45,—though Smith repudiates the theory in *The Philosophy of David Hume* (London: Macmillan, 1964) .

3. D. Hume, *The Letters of David Hume.* Ed. J. Y. T. Greig (Oxford: Oxford University Press, 1932) , 1:158.

4. *Enquiry,* p. 2.

less differ in aim and approach, and that a reading of
the *Enquiry* will implicitly convey everything of importance in the *Treatise*—except for an elaboration of
some points in their common epistemological theory. I
shall argue on independent grounds that the latter interpretation is more acceptable, but in any case, the cited
passages alone fail to establish the republication theory.

The second facet of external evidence looming large in
arguments for this theory has been a peculiar construction
placed on Hume's character and motives. Hume is portrayed as having been so consumed by literary ambition,
so dismayed at the failure of the *Treatise,* so ashamed at
having gone precipitately to press with that "juvenile
work," so thirsty for public approbation, and so sensitive
to criticism, that he determined to win acclaim by a
popular rehash of the *Treatise* in the *Enquiry*. To that
end "he set aside . . . even the consideration of truth"
(Kruse), gutted the *Treatise* of whatever he could not
popularise (Laing), amended some of its "imperfections
of structure . . . and extravaganzas" (Jessop), and added
some racy irrelevancies on religious topics to assure the
Enquiry of a wider public (Selby-Bigge). This characterization of Hume and of his literary practices purports
to be based on evidence culled both from his autobiographical sketch and from his correspondence; but it
ignores contrary evidence from the same sources. Thus,
for example, while critics frequently quote Hume's ad-
mission that his "love of literary fame [was his] ruling
passion," they tend less frequently to add his rider that
this "never soured [his] temper, notwithstanding [his]
frequent disappointments".[5] Even more rarely quoted is
the evidence from his letters that he was able to maintain

---

5. *Letters*, 1:2 ff.

about his lack of critical success a wry detachment: "I am now out of humour with myself; but doubt not, in a little time, to be only out of humour with the world like other unsuccessful authors."[6]

There is equally little justification for considering the *Treatise* to have been a "complete fiasco" (Kruse). While the book could hardly be described as a bestseller, and while Hume never lived to see the publication of the second edition, he expressed himself fairly satisfied with the trend in the sale of the *Treatise*.[7] Furthermore, recent historical research has shown that the allegation of a resounding critical silence at the first appearance of the *Treatise* is no longer tenable. Without pretending to arrive at a complete enumeration, E. C. Mossner cites some dozen English and Continental notices and reviews of the *Treatise*—not all unfavorable—in 1739 and 1740.[8] It was, therefore, not so much the quantity as the quality of critical attention that must have led to Hume's complaint regarding the still-birth of the *Treatise*.

There is also voluminous evidence in Hume's letters to Joseph Butler, Francis Hutcheson, William Mure, George Campbell, Lord Kames, and a number of Continental correspondents that, far from being sensitive to criticism, Hume actively sought it out. In the few cases where the criticism was cogent, Hume proved perfectly willing to amend and improve his doctrines or their presentation. Unfortunately, however, the largest part of the critical comment on the *Treatise* was uninformed, vituperative, or both. Where it was merely the first,

---

6. *Ibid.*, p. 30.
7. *Ibid.*, p. 37.
8. E. C. Mossner, "The First Answer to Hume's *Treatise*: An Unnoticed Item of 1740," *Journal of the History of Ideas*, 12 (1951) ; "The Continental Reception of Hume's *Treatise*, 1739–1741", *Mind*, 56 (1947) ; and *The Life of David Hume* (Edinburgh: Nelson, 1954) , pp. 117 ff.

Hume's reaction was one of studied politeness. Thomas Reid, for example, attacked Hume not for the cogency of his reasoning but for what he took to be the repugnant consequences of his doctrines.[9] For his part, Hume went out of his way to provide helpful comments on Reid's own work, even to the extent of correcting Reid's Scotticisms.[10] As for the more intemperate critics, Hume's wise policy was simply to ignore them: ". . . I am happy in my Resolution never to answer any of these People on any Occasion. For if I had ever been weak enough to have made any Reply to any Remarker, my Silence on this Occasion woud have been taken for a Conviction of Guilt."[11]

The imputation that differences between the *Treatise* and the *Enquiry* are to be explained by Hume's determination to curry favor with the crowd is inconsistent with the facts. On the one hand he is alleged to have omitted certain matters because "the general opinion would immediately have declared him an atheist" (Kruse) ; on the other, he included the Essay on Miracles, which he must have known would earn him precisely that epithet. That misdirected criticism had no influence on his writings is evidenced first by his own words: "Considering the Treatment I have met with, it woud have been very silly for me at my Years to continue writing any more; and still more blameable to warp my Principles and Sentiments

9. Reid, p. 115 n. and chapter 12. Norman Kemp Smith comments: "What Reid seems constantly to have had in mind when he thought of Hume was the teaching of the first twenty pages of Book I of the *Treatise* . . . . Everything else which Hume has to say is, Reid would seem to have held, exhaustively predetermined by these opening pages." ("David Hume: 1739–1939", *Proceedings of the Aristotelian Society*, supp. vol. 18 (1939) : xvii) .

10. *Letters*, 1:375 f.

11. D. Hume, *New Letters of David Hume*, ed. Klibansky and Mossner (Oxford: Oxford University Press, 1954) , pp. 60 f. For other references to his detractors, see *Letters*, 1:57, 59, 154, 164 f., 213, 222, 351, 510.

in conformity to the Prejudices of a stupid, factious Nation. . . ."[12] His integrity under the severest pressure is even better illustrated by the course of his life. Twice—in 1744 and again in 1751—Hume's applications for academic positions were rejected on the grounds of his "heresy, deism, scepticism, and atheism." When at last he obtained a reasonably comfortable position as librarian of the Advocates' Library in Edinburgh, one would expect from a servile pander such as Hume is portrayed to have been that he should quietly settle down to the writing of his *History* and steer clear of controversy. But this was not to be. When Hume was accused of acquiring objectionable literature for the library and put under the obligation of submitting future acquisitions for censorship, he made the reinstatement of the offending volumes a matter of principle. When he lost his case he resigned the post.[13] That Hume should disown his philosophical convictions "all for the approbation of the crowd" is simply beyond rational credence, if the man's act and word are to be given any weight.

So much, then, for the external evidence. The internal evidence is composed of a close comparison of the topics dealt with in both works, a comparison such as that undertaken by Selby-Bigge. But of course the comparison reveals that the *Enquiry* is not merely a republication of Book I of the *Treatise*. Large sections of the earlier work are omitted from the later; fully one third of the sections of the *Enquiry* break entirely new ground; and, where topics are common to both works, their treatment in the *Enquiry* differs significantly in emphasis and approach from that accorded them in the *Treatise*. The republica-

---

12. *Letters*, 2:269.
13. See J. Y. T. Greig, *David Hume* (London: Jonathan Cape, 1931), pp. 130 ff., 188 f., 190 ff., and comparable sections in Mossner's *Life*.

tionists recognize these disparities but explain them away as being dictated by exigencies of form or as being prudential suppressions or additions designed to evoke "a murmur among the zealots." This insistence on ulterior motives underlines the fact that, without this as an explanation, the substantial differences between the two works make it impossible for the one to be considered merely a republication of the other. It seems, therefore, reasonable to contend that if the motivational prop of the republication theory is too weak to bear the argument then the theory itself is rendered untenable.

The Revision Theory

The alternative to the republication theory may for convenience be labeled the revision theory.[14] One variation of this theory holds that in the years following the publication of the *Treatise* Hume became increasingly dissatisfied with the substantive doctrines of that work. The Appendix to the *Treatise* represents his first effort at revision, and the *Abstract*[15] his second. Finally, however, "the problem before him was not . . . one merely of minor repairs but . . . rather as to what could be sal-

---

14. It is advocated in various forms by C. W. Hendel, *Studies in the Philosophy of David Hume* (Princeton: Princeton University Press, 1925), chapter 4; J. A. Passmore, *Hume's Intentions* (Cambridge: Cambridge University Press, 1952), chapter 1; N. K. Smith, *The Philosophy of David Hume*, chapter 24, and "David Hume: 1739–1939"; A. Flew, *Hume's Philosophy of Belief* (London: Routledge and Kegan Paul, 1961), chapter 1, and "On the Interpretation of Hume," *Philosophy* 38 (1963); E. J. Furlong, "Imagination in Hume's *Treatise* and *Enquiry concerning the Human Understanding*", *Philosophy*, 36 (1961); H. H. Price, "The Permanent Significance of Hume's Philosophy," *Philosophy*, 15 (1940); R. Sternfeld, "The Unity of Hume's *Enquiry concerning Human Understanding*", *Review of Metaphysics* 3, no. 2 (undated reprint).

15. David Hume, *An Abstract of A Treatise of Human Nature*. Reprinted with an Introduction by Keynes and Sraffa (Cambridge: Cambridge University Press, 1938).

vaged from the wreckage" (Smith). Hence, nine years after the publication of Book I of the *Treatise* he undertook a more or less radical revision of its ontology and epistemology in the *Enquiry*. The similarities between the two works are explained by the fact that he was dealing with the same broad themes in both works and was thus able in some instances to salvage material from the *Treatise* and incorporate it in the *Enquiry*. Additions are thought to reflect advances in his thinking; and omissions reflect his reconsideration of "doctrines with which Hume had come to be profoundly dissatisfied, and which he could not, therefore—truth being still his quarry—allow himself to repeat" (Smith). The two works, though marked by some superficial similarities, are substantially different— a difference reflecting his rethinking of the positions adopted in the *Treatise* and a reconsideration of their consequences.

A variation of the revision theory considers that, while Hume "had 'completed' his logic . . . in the sense that its main principles were finally established in the *Treatise*" (Passmore), there were individual segments of his theory that he had reconsidered in the intervening years and that he was now eager to revise. Since the revisions were more radical than could be accommodated in a second edition of the original work, and since in any case the *Treatise* was marred by stylistic defects, Hume presented the fruits of his reconsiderations in a new work, the first *Enquiry*.

Like its rival, the revision theory is based on both textual and external evidence. It gains its credibility largely on account of the former, since in fact the two works differ substantially in content and even in their approach to a number of the topics which they do have ın common. However, the theory is not easily reconciled with Hume's explicit assertions to the effect that it was primarily the form of the *Treatise* with which he felt discontent, and even less so with his assertion that "the doctrines in both are the same." The contradiction can be reconciled only by motivational explanations. These, as in the case of similar exercises in support of the republication theory, fail to ring true. In the light of Hume's efforts to obtain critical comment on his work, and in the light of his frank admissions of error and puzzlement at seeming inconsistencies in his own work, it seems likely that had he wished to repudiate substantial portions of the *Treatise* he would, like Wittgenstein, have made his later work the vehicle of criticism against his earlier work.

The *Abstract* is taken as evidence of Hume's dissatisfaction with the *Treatise* and as an interim attempt to modify its doctrines. The *Abstract,* however, does not in fact presage a shift away from the general position of the *Treatise.* The interpretation it best lends itself to is that it is an attempt to clarify and draw attention to some salient epistemological features of the *Treatise.* This, indeed, is its avowed purpose; and in the absence of other than external—that is, motivational—evidence to the contrary, it does not seem justifiable for this stated and internally substantiated purpose to be ignored.[16]

If the republication theory founders on the differences between the two works, the radical revision theory founders on the remaining similarities between them. This is not to argue that Hume did not amend here and alter

---

16. See, for example, *Abstract*, preface and pp. 7, 8 ff., 19 ff., 23 f., 31. All these restate the doctrines of the *Treatise* substantially unchanged, complete even with what Hume recognized as their paradoxical consequences.

there. This he clearly did. But the job of revamping was not so thoroughgoing as to justify so uncompromising a view as Smith's: "Could Hume have obtained possession of every published copy of the *Treatise,* there can be no question that . . . he would have rejoiced to commit them to the flames."[17]

Each theory represents a plausible, if one-sided, attempt to solve a genuinely puzzling phenomenon—Hume's rewriting of what he had apparently intended to serve as a definitive epistemology. While they are agreed on the primary importance of the *Treatise* as a source for the exposition of this epistemology, the critics diverge in their views on the nature of the relationship of the *Enquiry* to the *Treatise.* The two theories discussed above are mutually incompatible; and evidence adduced in favor of one tends to conflict with, and cancel out, evidence in favor of the other. It is true that there is some republication of matter from the *Treatise* in the *Enquiry* and it is likewise true that the *Enquiry* revises some of the doctrines of the *Treatise;* but neither the thesis that the *Enquiry* is a substantial republication of the *Treatise* nor the thesis that it is a substantial revision of the *Treatise* seems capable of demonstration.

With neither view conclusively or even very convincingly established, it may be possible to develop a third theory as an alternative to both the republication and the revision theories. Such a theory would have to take into account all the evidence so far considered and, if possible, harmonize with Hume's views on the subject. Such an alternative is in fact available. It is examined in the next chapter, following the general reappraisal of the aim of the *Enquiry,* since the theory is closely linked to the conclusions of that reappraisal.

17. *The Philosophy of David Hume,* p. 532.

3
Ways of Knowing

The Aim of the First *Enquiry*

There is no lack of evidence, in books dealing with Hume, for Maund's thesis that a lack of sympathetic consideration and sometimes outright distortion of Hume's doctrines have played their part in creating the mystery surrounding aspects of Hume's philosophy. Others have noted that Hume's readers, perhaps Hume as well, were intellectual dilettantes and that this is why he failed to produce a clear and rigorous philosophy.[1] And indeed there is also no lack of evidence for this view. Section I of the *Enquiry* is an extended pledge to adhere as far as possible to an "easy and obvious" philosophy, and contains an apology for the occasional lapse into the "accurate and abstruse." Again, in subsequent sections, he all too frequently cuts short his discussion of vital points at the stage where

---

1. See, for example, S. N. Hampshire in *David Hume, a Symposium,* ed. D. F. Pears (London: Macmillan, 1963) , p. 3.

29

further investigation might call for some mental effort
from his readers:

> . . . I shall think it sufficient, if the present hints excite the
> curiosity of philosophers (sec. 4) ;
> . . . Should I multiply words about it, or throw it into a
> greater variety of lights, it would only become more obscure
> and intricate (sec. 7) ;
> But the state of the argument here proposed . . . will not
> disturb his ease by any intricate or obscure reasoning (sec. 8) ;
> But there occurs . . . a difficulty, which I shall just propose
> to you without insisting on it; lest it lead into reasonings of
> too nice and delicate a nature (sec. 11) ;
> It is sufficient to have dropped this hint at present, without
> prosecuting it any farther (sec. 12) .

Despite this attempt at simplification, which tends at
times to become oversimplification, the aim of the *Enquiry* is quite clearly expressed. It is to investigate not
this or that philosophical problem but rather to investigate the instrument employed in the investigation of
such problems. It is

> . . . to know the different operations of the mind, to separate
> them from each other, to class them under their proper heads,
> and to correct all that seeming disorder, in which they lie in-
> volved, when made the object of reflexion and enquiry. . . .
> And if we can go no farther than this mental geography, or
> delineation of the distinct parts and powers of the mind, it is
> at least a satisfaction to go so far. . . .
> It cannot be doubted, that the mind is endowed with sev-
> eral powers and faculties. . . . There are many obvious distinc-
> tions of this kind, such as those between the will and under-
> standing, the imagination and passions, which fall within
> the comprehension of every human creature. . . . And shall we
> esteem it worthy the labour of a philosopher to give us a true
> system of the planets, and adjust the position and order of
> those remote bodies; while we affect to overlook those, who,
> with so much success, delineate the parts of the mind, in which
> we are so intimately concerned?[2]

---

2. D. Hume, *Enquiries concerning the Human Understanding and*

This investigation he takes to be a necessary preliminary to any other intellectual endeavor. For it is only when we have established the competence, and the degree of competence, of a given faculty to investigate a particular cognitive object that we can have any confidence in the conclusions of our intellectual endeavors. To put this another way: it is necessary to assure that our investigative technique is appropriate to the object of investigation. Before applying, say, a battery of chemical tests to some object, we need to know that the tests are appropriate to the object. It would be futile to apply these chemical tests, say, to a problem in geometry.

The aim of the *Enquiry*, then, is to develop a faculty theory of knowledge—a mental geography—and the purpose of this theory is to inform us "what are the proper subjects of science and enquiry."[3] Failure to ascertain the scope and limits of the human understanding and its several faculties, failure to assure that the problem under investigation is investigated with the appropriate investigative technique, is "the justest and most plausible objection against a considerable part of metaphysics." This failure leads to "fruitless efforts of human vanity, which would penetrate into subjects utterly inaccessible to the understanding, or from the craft of popular superstitions . . . raise these intangling brambles to cover and protect their weakness."[4]

It is interesting to note that Hume does not pretend to account for the link between each faculty and its cognitive object. In the terms of his own comparison, his approach to the study of the human understanding is that of an

concerning the Principles of Morals, ed. L. A. Selby-Bigge, 2nd ed. (Oxford: Oxford University Press, 1902), pp. 13 f. See also *ibid.*, pp. 10, 12, 15, 163 ff.
3. *Ibid.*, p. 163.
4. *Ibid.*, p. 11.

anatomist.[5] He classifies the faculties as he finds them by introspection, and he goes on to describe the function when we are said to "reason justly." This is the scope and intention of his system, and it is to an exposition of that system that we now turn.

Outline of the "Mental Geography" or Faculty Theory of Knowledge

The means whereby we are to discover "what are the proper subjects of science and enquiry" is the mental geography. The geography comprises five cognitive faculties of the human understanding, and with each such faculty there is associated a cognitive sphere as its proper field of investigation. Hume holds each pair consisting of a faculty and a sphere to be inextricably linked. A given faculty is appropriate to one and only one field of enquiry, and a given field of enquiry is susceptible to the probing of one and only one faculty. It is only by correctly applying each given faculty to the appropriate field that man is able to investigate the phenomena or cognitive items coming within the ambit of human understanding.

The five faculties and their appropriate spheres of activity are, using largely Hume's terminology, the following: abstract reason, which is properly applied to relations of ideas; experimental reason, to matters of fact; perception, to percepts; (mental) taste or inclination, to value judgments; faith, to theology or divinity. Each series falls into two groups: the rational and the irrational. The former group, which includes abstract and experimental reason and their respective cognitive spheres, is characterized

---

5. *Ibid.*, p. 10.

by the fact that the appropriate inquiries are conducted by means of reasoning: that is, by educing conclusions from premises or from data by means of distinctive calculi. The latter group, which includes all the rest, is characterized by the fact that the appropriate investigations culminate in conclusions that are reached without an intervening calculating process but rather by a mental leap—something in the nature of direct inspection or introspection.

Most of the individual cognitive spheres are further subdivided. The whole system, comprising the human understanding and what it is fitted to investigate, can be set out in tabular form as on page 34.[6]

Much of the *Enquiry* develops the positive aspect of his theory. He investigates the correct procedures to be followed in examining specific questions with the appropriate mental faculty, and he explores the extent and nature of the positive information thus attainable. There are, thus, specific grounds on which we can justify an assertion to the effect that the diagonals of a parallelogram bisect each other or that whatever is long is not short. Similarly, there are means of establishing the probable validity of the claim that metals expand when heated or that there are craters on the hidden side of the moon. On a different plane and by different means we can also justify perceptual judgments; and it also makes sense to affirm that generosity is meritorious, that Masolino's frescoes are inspiring, or that sin is punished in the here-

6. I have tried where practicable to adhere to Hume's terminology. It will be noted that in one instance, "matters of fact," the generic and specific names of cognitive spheres coincide. Where he uses the same term to denote both faculty and sphere or where he has no generic sphere name at all, I have adopted modern equivalents. This has occurred in the case of "percepts" and "value judgments." "Tautologies" are not so designated by Hume but are discussed in the *Enquiry* on p. 163. For "rational faculties" Hume usually has "reason."

THE HUMAN UNDERSTANDING—AND ITS PROPER SUBJECTS

RATIONAL FACULTIES	ABSTRACT REASON	Relations of ideas	mathematics	arithmetic algebra geometry
			tautologies	
	EXPERIMENTAL REASON	Matters of fact	matters of fact	
			real existences	
	PERCEPTION	Percepts	impressions	sensations sentiments
			ideas	memory imagination
IRRATIONAL FACULTIES	TASTE	Value judgments	morals	
			criticism	
	FAITH	Theology		

after, all so long as the grounds for the assertion and the procedures of justification are appropriate to the case.[7]

However, the major portion of the *Enquiry* is concerned with the negative aspect of his theory. In this Hume is concerned with showing that the application of a mode of investigation to an inappropriate subject terminates in a negative result or in metaphysical error or in Pyrrhonic scepticism. We cannot, to use an analogy, expect to obtain correct information about a thing by examining it with the wrong instrument: we cannot study stars with a microscope, molecules with a telescope, or either with a stethoscope. It is so too with the exercise of the understanding. Considered by abstract reason, anything can be the cause of any other thing: in mathematics, the conclusions of experimental reason are paradoxical; moral arguments are incapable of supporting the religious hypothesis; and nothing but metaphysical nonsense ensues from the attempt to delve into "questions which lie entirely beyond the reach of human capacity."[8] The error in each of these cases, and in the many others considered by Hume, lies in subjecting the question under consideration "to such a trial as it is, by no means, fitted to endure."[9]

The negative aspect of Hume's epistemology was an attack on a variety of preceding and contemporaneous philosophies. Hume denied the rationalist doctrine that there is a universal a priori model of all knowledge, whether mathematical or factual, and he denied the then

---

7. In the main Hume speaks of "knowing," "feeling," "believing," and so forth in a transitive sense directed toward entities as the objects of, respectively, knowledge, sensation, and belief. There are other parts of the *Enquiry*, however, where he considers the objects of cognition as propositions. For examples of this, see *Enquiry* pp. 14, 25 f., 28, 95, 159.
8. The cited cases are discussed in *Enquiry*, pp. 25, 42, 156 f., 103, 81.
9. *Ibid.*, p. 130.

36   A FACULTY THEORY OF KNOWLEDGE

popular a posteriori argument for the existence of God.
Hume even provided an anticipatory rebuttal of Kant's
moral argument for the religious hypothesis. With his
insistence on the distinctness of varieties of argument
and on the limitation of each to its circumscribed field,
Hume foreshadowed the epistemology of the logical positivists and of Wittgenstein's *Tractatus*. But Hume's theory
was wider, more liberal, than those of his modern heirs;
for it allowed not only for analytic-deductive and syn-
thetic-verifiable propositions, but it also acknowledged as
meaningful propositions of value judgment and of theology, at least when derived by the appropriate methods.

Varieties of Understanding and Hume's Supposed Scepticism

Hume's reputation as a sceptic rests on an incorrect
or an incomplete reading of the *Enquiry*. True, Hume
does claim that we are assured that "our conclusions from
. . . experience are not founded on reasoning," that the
inference "from the cause to the effect proceeds not from
reason," that assent to the veracity of religion "is most
contrary to custom and experience," that belief in the
inherence of sensible qualities in material objects "carries
no rational evidence with it," that ethics and aesthetics
"are not to be controuled or altered by any philosophical
theory," and that a theological ethic leads to the "absurd
consequence" either that no action can be pronounced
evil or that God is accountable for the evil.[10] From such
assertions it is concluded that whatever Hume counts as
rationally untenable he advocates discarding as "nothing
but sophistry and illusion."[11]

10. *Ibid.*, pp. 32, 54, 131, 155, 103, 100.
11. *Ibid.*, p. 165.

The view that these theses reflect a radical scepticism is natural enough—but only if the relevant passages are torn from their context and if we disregard the important distinction he draws between the rational and the irrational. When Hume asserts, as he frequently does, that all reasoning is either abstract or experimental, he means precisely that: all *reasoning* is subsumed under one or the other of these categories. What he neither says nor means, but what he is frequently taken as meaning, is that he thereby excludes any other mode of understanding. In fact, not only does he consider phenomena that are beyond the pale of reason still to be in a sense knowable, but he even asserts that they are calculable—at least to the extent that these phenomena parallel, or form a compound with, "particular or general facts."[12] Were he to account irrational phenomena as being entirely beyond human ken, it would indeed reflect a radical scepticism, but it would also be quite contrary, among other things, to his explicitly nonsceptical theory of perception and his moral sense theory.

Evidence that the contrariety springs from critical misunderstanding rather than from Hume's disregard for consistency is provided in the closing three pages of the *Enquiry,* where he sums up the mental geography with respect to all the faculties and restates the central point: that what is cognizable becomes so by virtue of the correct application of the varieties of reason and other faculties to their proper spheres, while "nothing but sophistry and illusion" arise from the failure to limit inquiry within these proper bounds.

The form that this summary takes is an "examination into the natural powers of the human mind and . . . their

12. *Ibid.,* p. 165.

objects" so as to "find what are the proper subjects of
science and enquiry":

> Item, "The only objects of the abstract science or of demon-
> stration are quantity or number" and the express or elliptic
> tautologies contained in "all those pretended syllogistic reason-
> ings, which may be found in every other branch of learn-
> ing . . ."
> Item, "All other [rational] enquiries of men regard only
> matter of fact and existence . . . [which] can only be proved
> by arguments from its cause or its effect; and these arguments
> are founded entirely on experience, . . . which teaches us the
> nature and bounds of cause and effect, and enables us to infer
> the existence of one object from that of another."
> Item, "All other [perceptual] ideas are clearly distinct and
> different from each other, [and] we can never advance farther,
> by our utmost scrutiny, than to observe this diversity, and, by
> an obvious reflection, pronounce one thing not to be another."
> Item, "Morals and criticism are not so properly objects of
> the [rational] understanding as of taste and sentiment. . . . Or
> if we reason concerning it, and endeavour to fix its standard,
> we regard a new fact, to wit, the general tastes of mankind, or
> some such fact, which may be the object of reasoning and
> enquiry."
> Item, "Theology . . . has a foundation in *reason,* so far as
> it is supported by experience. But its best and most solid foun-
> dation is *faith* and divine revelation."[13]

Viewed in this context, the concluding peroration takes
on a new meaning:

> When we run over libraries, persuaded of these principles,
> what havoc must we make? If we take in our hand any vol-
> ume; of divinity or school metaphysics, for instance; let us
> ask, *Does it contain any abstract reasoning concerning quan-
> tity or number?* No. *Does it contain any experimental reason-
> ing concerning matter of fact and existence?* No. Commit it
> then to the flames: for it can contain nothing but sophistry
> and illusion.[14]

---

13. *Ibid.,* pp. 163 ff.
14. *Ibid.,* p. 165.

This does not advocate—as Hume's critics almost unanimously take it to do—the indiscriminate incineration of works of divinity or school metaphysics.[15] What it does in fact recommend is the rejection of those theories that derive from abstract arguments regarding matters other than those appropriate to deductive demonstration, or from experimental arguments regarding matters other than those appropriate to inductive inference.

This, then, sums up Hume's mental geography and its conclusions. As a result of the general neglect of, or the secondary status accorded to, the *Enquiry,* no complete account of this doctrine has ever been provided by Hume's critics and commentators. The few who have taken any cognizance of it at all have given incomplete or distorted versions by enumerating only some of the faculties or confusing generic and specific cognitive spheres or amending Hume's doctrine to fit some personal preconception or theory. Flew, for example, asserts that Hume draws his map of mental geography with a two-pronged "Fork," comprising abstract and experimental reasoning.[16] Constance Maund attributes to Hume a theory comprising a fourfold division of cognitive objects: impressions, ideas, and the objects of abstract and experimental reason.[17] N. K. Smith finds Hume's theory to imply a threefold distinction between immediate awareness, deductive knowl-

---

15. A. Flew, *Hume's Philosophy of Belief* (London: Routledge and Kegan Paul, 1961) , p. 273; J. A. Passmore, *Hume's Intentions* (Cambridge University Press, 1952) , p. 65; A. H. Basson, *David Hume* (Harmondsworth: Penguin Books, 1958) , p. 150; Farhang Zabeeh, *Hume: Precursor of Modern Empiricism* (The Hague: Martinus Nijhoff, 1960) , p. 28 f.; G. E. Moore, "Hume's Philosophy" in *Philosophical Studies* (London: Routledge and Kegan Paul, 1922) , p. 164; J. O. Urmson, *Philosophical Analysis: Its Development between the Two World Wars* (Oxford: Oxford University Press, 1956) , p. 102.

16. Flew, *Hume's Philosophy of Belief,* chapter 3 and pp. 270 f.

17. C. Maund, *Hume's Theory of Knowledge* (London: Macmillan, 1937) , pp. 27 ff.

edge, and inferential belief.[18] And MacNabb presents
Hume's mental geography as stipulating four distinct ways
of knowing: by perception, by memory, by demonstration,
and by probable reasoning.[19] While these theses may be
an improvement on Hume, they do not seem to me to
represent what they claim to be, namely the doctrine
actually expounded by Hume.

The Treatise and the Enquiry: the Complementary Theory

If it is granted that the *Enquiry* develops a faculty
theory of knowledge along the lines I have proposed in
the preceding pages, we shall be in a better position to
appreciate the independent importance of the *Enquiry*
and to understand the relation between that work and
the *Treatise*. Its importance lies in the fact that Hume
nowhere else gives a complete, systematic account of this
theory; hence it is to the *Enquiry* that we must turn for
an insight into this aspect of his philosophy. With regard
to the other point, a digressive examination of textual
and biographical evidence is necessary.

In his correspondence,[20] Hume tells how at the age of
eighteen "there seemed to be opened up to him a new
scene of thought which transported him beyond measure."
He had discovered a medium wherewith to terminate "all
those endless disputes even in the most fundamental
articles of philosophy." Hume's inspiration sprang from
the observation that the deficiencies of philosophy were

---

18. N. K. Smith, *The Philosophy of David Hume* (London: Macmillan, 1964), chapter 15.
19. D. G. C. MacNabb, *David Hume: His Theory of Knowledge and Morality* (London: Hutchinson's University Library, 1951), chapter 3.
20. *The Letters of David Hume*, 1: 13.

not so much due to illicit argument in detail as to erroneous methodology. The main form that this error assumed was the indiscriminate application of deductive reasoning, which had proved successful in one sphere of inquiry, to other spheres where it had no applicability at all. That mathematical problems and syllogistic conundrums had yielded to deductive methods of approach was taken as a ground for attempting the deductive proof of the existence of the self or of angels, and of the circularity of celestial orbits, and of this or that moral system.

In daily life, Hume argued, factual and existential matters are determined by reference not to deductive principles but to "experience" and "analogy." He contended that, since we are so psychologically framed that this is how in fact such matters are determined, it is by reference to "experience" and "analogy" that factual and existential problems in philosophy are also to be resolved. It was not, for Hume, a matter of the intrinsic nature of synthetic as against that of analytic propositions that made the former incapable of demonstrative proof. It was, rather, a factor inhering in human nature: we accept the truth of an analytic proposition because its contradictory is not humanly conceivable; and, by the same token, we cannot treat a synthetic proposition as necessarily true because its contradictory is humanly conceivable. Hence it is that the *Treatise* is a *Treatise of Human Nature:* the problems of philosophical methodology are rooted in human nature, and they are subject to its limitations.[21]

Hume does not limit himself, however, to what Flew has called Hume's Fork. He considers that there are alternatives to deductivism other than argument from

21. See D. Hume, *An Abstract of A Treatise of Human Nature,* ed. Keynes and Sraffa (Cambridge: Cambridge University Press, 1938) , p. 7 and *passim.*

experience and analogy. Thus, there appear in the *Treatise* rather full accounts of perceptual experience and of the moral sense. However, his main aims in that work are two. First, he wishes to show the limited applicability of abstract reason. Second, and more important, he wishes to subject hitherto unresolved questions of philosophy to the mode of investigation he calls experimental reason. His preoccupation with these aims is evidenced by the fact that the bulk of the *Treatise* is taken up with the investigation by experimental reason of these very problems. The outstanding feature of his treatment of these questions is the detailed exploration not only of the licit bounds of experimental reason but also of its limitations. These are manifested in the contradictions, absurdities, and paradoxes that arise when these limitations are transcended. This is the source of the notorious sceptical conclusions concerning space and time, material objects and personal identity, even reason and the senses themselves. But these conclusions need not and, I believe, do not represent Hume's position; rather they arise from the very scope of the *Treatise,* the analysis in various fields of conclusions arising from the application of experimental reason.[22]

---

22. I believe there is an illuminating analogy between the sceptical conclusions of Hume in the *Treatise* and those of Kant in *Religion within the Bounds of Pure Reason* (1793). There Kant examines three speculative arguments for the existence of God: the ontological argument, the cosmological argument, and the argument from design. He finds that each of the three fails and concludes therefrom that speculative theology is a tissue of errors. Similarly, Hume concludes in the *Treatise* that, so far as certain types of reason are concerned, there are no grounds for asserting the infinite divisibility of time and space, for believing in external existences, or for entertaining the notion of personal identity. But neither Kant nor Hume insisted on the finality of these negative conclusions. What both did insist on was that the negative conclusions followed from given premises considered in a certain light.

Had Kant written nothing further on the theological problem, he would have been accounted an agnostic: but this, of course, was not his

The nature of the criticism that the *Treatise* attracted persuaded Hume that he had failed not only in effecting the desired methodological revolution but even in achieving comprehensibility. For this Hume accepted the blame, attributing it not so much to the matter of the *Treatise* as to the manner in which its doctrines had been presented. However, that the alleged formal defects had little to do with stylistic niceties is intimated by that work's continued reputation as a superb example of eighteenth-century prose. And that lack of comprehension for the *Treatise* was also not due to excessive prolixity is attested by the remarkable economy of treatment of many of its major topics: four pages on "Of Knowledge," two on "Of Relations," one and a half on "Of Modes and Substances," and so forth. The length of the *Treatise* is a function not of the detailed or repetitious treatment of any single topic, but rather of the number of topics covered. This, however, is unexceptionable in a book purporting to examine the conclusions of experimental reason over so wide a field of topics as is comprised by the category of "moral subjects."

Indeed, the only specific defect that Hume explicitly deplores is "the positive Air, which prevails in that Book, and which may be imputed to the Ardour of Youth."[23] This refers to what does in fact constitute the major shortcoming of the *Treatise:* his positive assertion of

---

final position. Neither was the ontological agnosticism of the *Treatise* Hume's final position. That Hume was indignant at the thought that this should be taken as the interpretation of his doctrines is well illustrated by his remark in a letter to John Stewart: "But allow me to tell you, that I never asserted so absurd a Proposition as *that any thing might arise without a Cause*: I only maintain'd, that our Certainty of the Falsehood of that Proposition proceeded neither from Intuition nor Demonstration; but from another Source. . . . There are many different kinds of Certainty; and some of them as satisfactory to the Mind, tho perhaps not so regular, as the demonstrative kind." (*Letters* 1: 187) .

23. *Letters*. 1: 187.

philosophical conclusions without the provision of an
adequate or systematic account of the assumptions on
which these conclusions are based. The *Treatise* is the
application of an epistemological theory, or of parts of
such a theory; but of the theory itself the reader is left
largely in the dark.

It was this gap that the *Enquiry* seems to have been designed to fill. In it Hume passed from the proliferation of
instances to the construction of the theory that accommo-
dates these instances. Although some of the illustrative
examples of the *Treatise* are retained, many others can
now be omitted to make room for a more thorough
presentation of the foundations of his theory. Hence his
claim, *"Addo dum minuo."*[24] This view of the *Enquiry*
as complementing and explaining the doctrines of the
earlier work also makes sense of his assertion that "the
philosophical Principles are the same in both";[25] the
Enquiry makes explicit the same principles that the *Treatise* assumes and applies. Again, the complementary theory
provides some reason and justification—besides wounded
vanity—for his advice against the reading of the *Treatise*.
For unless the doctrines of that work are carefully considered in the light of the epistemological theory of the
Enquiry, they are subject to the kind of misinterpretation
represented by the reduction of his theory of the understanding to two faculties, or by the sceptical conclusions
which are attributed to him and which he consistently
denied as representing more than the conclusions of certain rationalist practices.

The republication and revision theories discussed in
chapter 2 derive their credibility from the fact that the

24. *Ibid.,* p. 158.
25. *Ibid.,* p. 158.

Enquiry does contain some republication and some revision of doctrines first proposed in the *Treatise*. But each theory focuses on only one of these aspects of the *Enquiry*. The fact that both aspects feature in the *Enquiry* with sufficient prominence to support either theory indicates that neither predominates to the exclusion of the other. Equal attention given to both the similarities and the differences between the two works suggests that the similarities stem from their common epistemological basis in Hume's faculty theory of knowledge, and the differences from the fact that the *Treatise* consists largely of the consequences of the faculty theory of knowledge while the *Enquiry* consists largely of its premises.

4
Abstract Reason

The Mode of Exposition

Since Hume's system comprises five faculties, each of which can appropriately or otherwise be applied to any of five major cognitive spheres, there are theoretically twenty-five distinct areas which together make up the terrain to be charted by the mental geography. Of this number only a few represent what to Hume is a permissible exercise of the faculties. The rest transcend the legitimate bounds within which the human understanding can be exercised. Hume marks this distinction either by explicit reference to "just reasoning" and its contrary or by exposing the paradoxical or otherwise untenable consequences that arise when a faculty is misapplied.

There are two possible approaches to the exposition of the type of faculty theory contained in the *Enquiry*. The first is to take in turn each of the cognitive spheres and to investigate the extent to which the various faculties are applicable to it. The second is to start with the faculties and attempt to apply each in turn to the various cognitive spheres. The end result of either approach will be the systematic examination of each of the modes obtained by applying five faculties to five cognitive spheres. The usual practice in the exegesis of Hume has been a partial exposition along the former lines; and Hume's approach has been along the same lines. In Hume's case, this approach seems to have been dictated by his predilection for making his points through the medium of illustrative examples. He has generally taken a problem typical to a sphere of enquiry—the existence of God or of material objects, the validation of probabilistic judgments, freedom of the will, and the like—and examined the nature and the extent of information that can be obtained on such a problem by various methods of enquiry. After claiming to show that certain methods terminate in paradoxical conclusions and others in neutral conclusions, he argues that the remaining method is the only one appropriate to the question at all.

While there is no inherent disadvantage in the first approach, the second has been adopted in the present instance. By this approach it is hoped, first, to overcome the tendency to treat what are essentially illustrative examples as the major aspect of his epistemology. It is true that the conclusions regarding the individual cases are intrinsically important, and the critical attention lavished on them attests to their importance; but it is also true that these individual cases have tended to obscure the perspective of his epistemology as a whole. Second, it is hoped to rectify misunderstandings of the individual doctrines arising, in part, from this failure to relate them to his faculty theory. Third, it is hoped that this approach will throw into sharper relief the nature of his epistemology as a faculty theory of knowledge. Hence in the present work the usual method of exposition is reversed, and it is the faculties that are given a central place. In the rest of this chapter we shall be concerned with the faculty of abstract reason and its relation to the various cognitive spheres.

Abstract Reason and Relations of Ideas

Hume's criteria for distinguishing between the propositions of abstract reason and those of experimental reason include elements from the criteria for distinguishing among the propositions of two other dichotomies adopted in later empirical systems: the a priori-a posteriori dichotomy and the analytic-synthetic dichotomy. However, since Hume's aversion to "abstruse philosophy" led to the omission of any systematic account of these criteria, the following remarks can claim to be no more than a reconstruction of this aspect of his doctrine from the "hints" with which he hoped to "excite the curiosity of philosophers."

The first criterion is what may be termed the aprioristic criterion. What distinguishes the propositions of abstract reason is that they are "discoverable by the mere operation of thought, without dependence on what is anywhere existent in the universe."[1] In his disquisition on the infinitesimal calculus,[2] Hume goes even further

1. D. Hume, *Enquiries concerning the Human Understanding and concerning the Principles of Morals*, ed. L. A. Selby-Bigge, 2nd ed. (Oxford: Oxford University Press, 1902), p. 25.

2. *Ibid.*, pp. 156 ff.

than to suggest the independence of abstract reason from empirical tests: he claims that there exists an incompatibility between the conclusions of abstract and of experimental reason when applied to the same problem. The point there under discussion is the quantitative valuation of the angle of contact between a circle and its tangent. In Leibnizian calculus, any such angle, which is initially infinitely smaller than a right angle, continues to decrease infinitesimally in proportion to an increase in the diameter of the circle. Considered abstractly, Hume asserts, the argument whereby this is proved seems "unexceptionable"; but applied to spatial figures the conclusion is "big with contradiction and absurdity." (In modern mathematics, the angle under discussion is simply taken as equal to zero.) Hume's reasoning, here as elsewhere, is along the line that what may validly be asserted of concepts or entities in one sphere cannot be transposed to another by the mere substitution of terms.

The first criterion is in turn made dependent on another: what makes abstract propositions knowable a priori is their analyticity.[3] Mathematical propositions, for example, are true because their conclusions are already "contained" in the premises. The mathematical propositions which Hume discusses in this connection are equations. A second variety of abstractly true proposition is the verbal tautology, which depends for its truth on a special species of analyticity: the equation of the subject and the predicate by definition. "But to convince us of this proposition, *that where there is no property, there can be no injustice,* it is only necessary to define the terms, and explain injustice to be a violation of property."[4]

---

3. *Ibid.*, pp. 37 and 163.
4. *Ibid.*, p. 163.

The principle of analyticity is, in its turn, made to rest on yet a third criterion, the law of contradiction.[5] If the negation of a proposition is self-contradictory, then its affirmation is abstractly true; if not, then the proposition is not subject to abstract validation by the test of analyticity.

We have, thus, a hierarchy of criteria. The abstract is what can be known a priori; the a priori is what is analytic; and the analytic is true by virtue of the law of contradiction.

Occasionally Hume introduces a fourth criterion which is sometimes allied to, and sometimes identified with, the law of contradiction. This criterion is the inconceivability of opposites.[6] If a state of affairs, opposite that expressed by a proposition, cannot be conceived (presumably as a perceptual idea or mental image), then the proposition affirming the state of affairs is formally true and hence one of abstract reason; if the opposite is conceivable, the proposition is not formally true and hence not one of abstract reason. Like the law of contradiction, this is proffered as a test of analyticity. Unlike that law, however, it does not express a logical relation; rather it describes an alleged psychological fact.

The object of abstract reason is that science, or propositions expressing the content of that science, which meet the requirements of the criteria. Hume's generic name for this science is "relations of ideas," a term under which are subsumed the three traditional branches of mathematics and, as a separate species, syllogistic logic.[7] Hume excludes all nonanalytic propositions from the scope of abstract reason, both implicitly by the application of his

5. *Ibid.*, pp. 18 and 164.
6. *Ibid.*, pp. 26 and 164.
7. *Ibid.*, pp. 25, 31, 108, 163.

criteria and explicitly by the express limitation of what counts as relations of ideas to these species. Although other propositions are thereby automatically excluded, much of the *Enquiry* is nevertheless devoted to detailed arguments for the inapplicability of abstract calculus to these excluded propositions and to an exposition of the fallacies that arise from any such misapplication. His procedure is to select propositional and situational paradigms in each of the excluded spheres and to generalize from the paradigm to the whole sphere.

Abstract Reason and Matters of Fact

The cognitive sphere designated by the generic term "matters of fact" coincides with the logical positivist category of empirical or synthetic propositions,[8] except that Hume's genus excludes propositions relating to the varieties of perception. Among matters of fact Hume distinguishes two species: "matters of fact" and "real existences". The latter species comprises existential propositions of the type "x exists"; the former, predicative assertions regarding that which is said to exist. This distinction is not fully developed by Hume, and the identity of generic and specific names further obscures his argument. However, that he intends to draw some such distinction is indicated by those passages where he mentions the species jointly without the suggestion that they are alternative names, and by other passages where he considers one as specifically distinct from the other.[9] That most of his discussion of the inapplicability of abstract reason to

8. See for example A. J. Ayer, *Language, Truth, and Logic*, 2nd ed. (London: Victor Gollancz, 1964), pp. 9 f. and 78 f.
9. For example, *Enquiry*, pp. 26, 35, 164.

nonanalytic assertions is centered on its inapplicability to empirical propositions arises from the prevalence in his time of speculative systems claiming to be based on self-evident premises and valid inferences on subjects such as "those concerning the origin of worlds, or the economy of the intellectual system or region of spirits, . . . and the situation of nature, from, and to eternity".[10] The *Enquiry* is, therefore, particularly rich in matter-of-fact paradigms.[11]

The development of his argument from these paradigms is highly ramified and complex. In the first instance, he attempts to relate all generically factual propositions to a single paradigmatic proposition—the causal maxim. This reduction includes both existential and predicative propositions:

> . . . All our evidence for any matter of fact, which lies beyond the testimony of sense or memory, is derived entirely from the relation of cause and effect.
>
> The existence, therefore, of any being can only be proved by arguments from its cause or its effect.[12]

In the second instance, he attempts by means of logical argument, illustrative example, and psychological description to show that the causal maxim—and hence the factual and existential propositions which depend on it—can not be deductively derived.

Given the correctness of his analysis of abstract reason, "Hume's deathblow to deductivism"[13] can be more briefly and simply stated. If a priori knowledge depends on analyticity, and analyticity depends on the law of contradiction, it follows that neither existential nor matter-of-

---

10. *Ibid.*, pp. 81 and 162.
11. *Ibid.*, pp. 29, 32, 33, 43, 45, 53, 54, 87, 89, and others.
12. *Ibid.*, pp. 159 and 164. The subordinate clause in the first passage is intended to exclude "perceptual" propositions from the discussion.
13. The title of an article by D. S. Miller in *Journal of Philosophy*, 46 (1949).

fact propositions can be affirmed on a priori grounds. The negation of propositions of the type "*x* is *φ*" and "*x* exists" is not self contradictory; hence the affirmation is contingent.

Neither Hume's reduction of empirical propositions to the causal maxim nor the extra-logical arguments are essential to his case. In fact, they tend to obscure the very point that they are intended to reinforce. Of course, that point is itself explicitly stated by Hume:

> That there are no demonstrative arguments for the assertion that like sensible qualities must always be attended with like secret powers seems evident; since it implies no contradiction that the course of nature may change, and that an object, seemingly like those which we have experienced, may be attended with different or contrary effects.[14]
>
> When a man says, *I have found, in all past instances, such sensible qualities conjoined with such secret powers:* And when he says, *Similar sensible qualities will always be conjoined with similar secret powers,* he is not guilty of a tautology.
>
> If we reason *a priori,* anything may appear able to produce anything.[15]

The whole doctrine concerning the inapplicability of abstract reason to matters of fact is summed up in the dicta: "Whatever *is* may *not be*" and "No negation of a fact can involve a contradiction."[16]

Critique of Hume's Theory of Abstract Reason and the Objects of Rational Knowledge

At this point we may briefly examine some of the types of criticism leveled at Hume's analysis of the relation of abstract reason to the two rational cognitive spheres. First

---

14. *Enquiry,* pp. 34 f.
15. *Ibid.,* pp. 37 and 164.
16. *Ibid.,* p. 164.

to be considered is Quine's suggestion that the analytic-synthetic dichotomy is itself nothing more than "an unempirical dogma of empiricists, a metaphysical article of faith."[17] Instead of an exhaustive and mutually exclusive division of propositions into necessary and contingent classes, Quine offers a graded and constantly ratifiable scale of propositional values. His rejection of the traditional propositional categories rests essentially on a criticism of their criteria: verifiability in the case of synthetic propositions and synonymy in the case of analytic propositions. Since there seems to be no satisfactory way of making sense of these basic notions, the categories which ultimately rest on them are themselves untenable. A further criticism of analyticity, according to Quine, arises from its failure to satisfy the primary requirement demanded of it: that its conclusions be immune from revision. Yesterday's indubitable deductive truths are today's controvertible hypotheses. The dichotomy is therefore not only invalid, but it is also useless for arriving at the certainties which it promises to provide.

Quine's argument and his subsequent developments of the theme have at least so much force that it is no longer possible to consider the traditional propositional categories as universally valid absolutes. However, I agree with Putnam[18] that the dichotomy can survive in an amended form: that is, as a stipulation convenient for, and valid within, an axiomatic system. To the question whether we wish a discredited concept to survive in any form, I think the answer is yes. This is so because the analytic-synthetic dichotomy happens to provide us with a

---

17. W. V. O. Quine, *From a Logical Point of View* (Cambridge, Mass.: Harvard University Press, 1953) , p. 37.

18. H. Putnam, "The Analytic and the Synthetic", *Minnesota Studies in the Philosophy of Science*, vol. 3, ed. Feigl and Maxwell (Minneapolis: University of Minnesota Press, 1962) .

convenient distinction, at least for the purpose of formal languages, between statements that are regarded as axiomatic—that is, immune from revision within the system —and those that are regarded as not immune from revision. And it is true today, as it was in Hume's time, that such a distinction provides a useful operational tool in logic and mathematics.

It may also be that Quine's requirements for the determinacy of the expressions in the dichotomy are too stringent. There is in logic no stronger and no weaker a basis for any other possible distinction than there is for that between analytic and synthetic propositions. What this suggests is that perhaps all distinctions are conventional: but while the absence of a logical basis for a distinction may prevent that distinction from being regarded as a transcendental absolute, it need not prevent it from being used within a logically defined system.

Lastly, even if we are unable to arrive at a satisfactory definition of analyticity or any of its criteria, we are thereby neither assured that no such definition is obtainable nor debarred from using the category undefined. We may sidestep the issue of definition by stipulating the conditions of its use as an undefined operator in a logical system. Such a logic incorporating analytic propositions provides us, if not with immutable truths, at least with a symbolic convention "allowing us to use pairs of expressions inter-changeably"[19] or to "pronounce one thing not to be another."[20]

A second criticism directed at Hume is the contention that he does not in the proper sense provide a philosophical solution to an epistemological problem. His entire

---

19. Putnam, p. 396. See also J. Bennett, "Analytic-Synthetic," *Proceedings of the Artistotelian Society* 59 (1958-59).
20. *Enquiry*, p. 163.

discourse amounts to no more than a psychological description of what allegedly occurs when we engage in cognitive activity.[21] Hume might be excused, however, though his doctrine cannot be vindicated, on the historical ground that there was no clear conceptual or methodological demarcation between epistemology and psychology in his day. The more constructive critics have suggested that something can be salvaged from his doctrine if we make the appropriate logical substitutions for Hume's psychological terminology. Thus we might read "stipulative" and "derivative" for Hume's "intuitive" and "demonstrative" truths and, following Passmore, "things" and "empirical propositions" for Hume's "impressions" and "beliefs." In fact, however, although Hume's statement cannot be regarded as a rigorous logical exposition, he has himself provided in many instances epistemological equivalents for what he elsewhere treats in psychological terms.[22]

A third criticism to be considered involves the claim that Hume errs in excluding from the province of abstract reason all matters of fact, and the claim consequent on

21. Ayer, pp. 137 f.; R. W. Church, *Hume's Theory of the Understanding* (London: George Allen & Unwin, 1935), p. 11; A. Flew, *Hume's Philosophy of Belief* (London: Routledge and Kegan Paul, 1961), pp. 117 ff. and 211; T. E. Jessop, "Some Misunderstandings of Hume," *Revue Internationale de Philosophie* 6 (1952) : 160; H. H. Price, *Hume's Theory of the External World* (Oxford: Oxford University Press, 1940), p. 14; F. Zabeeh, *Hume: Precursor of Modern Empiricism* (The Hague: Martinus Nijhoff, 1960), p. 158; J. A. Passmore, *Hume's Intentions* (Cambridge: Cambridge University Press), pp. 18, 77, 155 ff.; H. Reichenbach, "On the Justification of Induction," in *Readings in Philosophical Analysis*, ed. Feigl and Sellars (New York: Appleton-Century-Crofts, 1949), p. 325; G. Santayana, *Scepticism and Animal Faith* (London: Constable, 1923), p. 295.

22. For opposing views on whether alternative languages can generate conceptual equivalences, see for example A. J. Ayer, *The Foundations of Empirical Knowledge* (London: Macmillan, 1963), chapter 5, and the appendix to R. M. Chisholm, *Perceiving* (Ithaca, N. Y.: Cornell University Press, 1957).

this that some matters of fact can be known abstractly. This question has been approached from many sides: as the problem of predictability, as the problem of providing justification for theories of probability, as the possibility of logical argument from past to future, from the observed to the unobserved, from the known to the unknown, from a sample to the whole species, and from a sample to another sample within a species. It opens up the whole immensely complex and ramified question of the justification of induction. It is not within the scope of the present book to examine the solutions proposed to this problem; but since much of what has been written on the subject takes Hume as a starting point, and since writers who affirm the possibility of a positive solution commence by invalidating Hume's doctrine, I intend here to indicate the lines of attack against Hume and briefly to evaluate the cogency of these lines.

The naïve causalism of the dialectical materialist relies on the argument that deliberate human manipulation of nature and successful prediction of physical experiment or of astronomical calculation prove the objectivity of causality as an operative factor in nature. Engels, who uses such an argument, considers that abortive experiments even provide additional support for causalism: "It is precisely this which *proves* causality instead of refuting it, because we can find out the cause of each such deviation from the rule by appropriate investigation . . . so that here the test of causality is so to say a *double* one."[23]

Apart from the fact that Engels is driven in a subsequent passage to concede that Hume's scepticism was

23. F. Engels, *Dialectics of Nature*, 3rd rev. ed. (Moscow: Progress Publishers, 1964), pp. 233 f. See also, by the same author, "Ludwig Feuerbach and the End of Classical German Philosophy," in Marx and Engels, *On Religion* (Moscow: Foreign Languages Publishing House, 1955).

correct in saying that a regular *post hoc* can never establish a *propter hoc,* this variety of naïve causalism misses the point of Hume's analysis. For Hume's doctrine is not concerned with subverting the objectivity or the success of causally predicated prediction: "I have never asserted so absurd a Proposition as *that any thing might arise without a Cause.*"[24] What he is concerned with, at least in the negative sense, is to establish broadly what Engels has conceded: that in reasoning from the known to the unknown, from the past to the future, "there is a certain step taken; a process of thought, and an inference, which wants to be explained"; and that "the knowledge of this relation is not, in any instance, attained by reasonings *a priori.*"[25]

An allied if somewhat more sophisticated criticism of Hume's doctrine is what we may call the alternative cosmology argument. It springs from a rejection of Hume's theory of perception and, in particular, of that part of the theory which argues for the logical independence of each percept from any other percept. It is this "kaleidoscopism" that is seen as the major barrier to conceiving the universe as an ordered entity regulated by discoverable laws and subject to a predictive calculus. In order to permit such a calculus to operate, alternative cosmologists argue that the possibility of logical entailment among events must be postulated. Thomas Reid, for example, introduces such a postulate by declaring the causal maxim to be one of "three first principles of necessary truths."[26]

---

24. D. Hume, *The Letters of David Hume*; ed. J. Y. T. Greig (Oxford: Oxford University Press, 1932) , 1: 185 ff.

25. *Enquiry*, pp. 33 f. and 27.

26. T. Reid, *Essays on the Intellectual Powers of Man*, ed. A. D. Woozley (London: Macmillan, 1941) , pp. 396 ff. The other two principles affirm the reality of matter and of mind and the deducibility of intelligent purpose from the design of the universe.

Modern alternative cosmologists use the same stipulative technique. Thus Hartshorne claims that, since we do in fact rely on inductive prediction and since we have no better method of dealing with the future, we must adopt as an axiom the logical dependence of events upon their predecessors; and Whitehead argues for such a postulate as a "necessary preliminary, if we are to justify induction."[27]

The alternative cosmology argument does not attempt to refute Hume: in fact it admits that, given perceptual kaleidoscopism, "Hume's argument concerning induction is irrefutable."[28] What it does is to plead that the consequences of Hume's theory are repugnant and that an alternative cosmology is necessary to save science from scepticism:

> If the cause in itself discloses no information as to the effect, so that the first invention of it must be *entirely* arbitrary, it follows at once that science is impossible, except in the sense of establishing *entirely arbitrary* connections which are not warranted by anything intrinsic to the natures either of causes or effects. . . . But scientific faith has risen to the occasion, and has tacitly removed the philosophic mountain.[29]

The sort of theory that Whitehead believes is saved by scientific faith is contained in the following passage:

> The issue of the combined labours of Galileo, Newton, Descartes, and Huygens has some right to be considered as the greatest single intellectual success which mankind has achieved. In estimating its size, we must consider the complete-

27. C. Hartshorne, "Hume's Metaphysics and Its Present-Day Influence," *The New Scholasticism* 25 (1961) : 162, and A. N. Whitehead, *Science and the Modern World* (New York: New American Library, 1948), pp. 4 and 44.
28. M. W. Gross, "Whitehead's Answer to Hume," *Journal of Philosophy*, 38 (1941) : 95–102.
29. Whitehead, p. 4.

ness of its range. It constructs for us a vision of the material universe, and it enables us to calculate the minutest detail of a particular occurrence.[30]

The rejection of Hume's theory on such grounds as Whitehead's seems unjustified, first, because the question of the consequence of a theory is distinct from that of its validity. Second, even if the consequence is such as Whitehead suggests, and even if this is a relevant issue, then that question—as far as one school of modern science is concerned—has been settled in favor of Hume. J. Robert Oppenheimer sums it up in these words:

> Quantum theory is, of course, an acausal theory in the sense that events happen for which no precise cause can be determined or given. A given nucleus disintegrates at three o'clock on the afternoon of a certain day. No one in the world could find out when that would happen until it did happen. . . . It is a nondeterminist theory. There is no possibility, as there was in Laplace's nightmare, of knowing everything about the world right now—not a very plausible assumption—and therefore knowing all about its future—not a very happy outcome. . . . Everything about this is quite different from the Newtonian picture.[31]

What is important about the acausalism of quantum theory is that the unpredictability of physical events (beyond statistical probability) is not merely the result of incomplete knowledge. That is, it cannot be argued that we could foretell the disintegration of a given nucleus at a particular instant in the future if only we had sufficient knowledge of the state of the universe at present. Such absolute predictability is impossible even in theory because, in quantum mechanics, the "attributes of physical

---

30. *Ibid.,* p. 47.
31. R. J. Oppenheimer, *The Flying Trapeze: Three Crises for Physicists* (London: Oxford University Press, 1964) , p. 53.

objects can no longer be given absolute content. . . . A characteristic feature of the quantum mechanical description is that the representation of a state of a system can never imply the accurate determination of both members of a pair of conjugate variables p and q." For the physicist, therefore, science does not require to be saved from Hume's criticism of the a priori causal principle. In fact, the discovery of the universal quantum of action "is not only foreign to the classical theories of mechanics and electromagnetism, but is even irreconcilable with the very idea of causality."[32]

A different attempt to reestablish the a priorism of induction is represented by the argument for an analytic relationship between the premises and the conclusion in an inductive argument. Of several attempts at such a propositional solution, one of the most fully evolved is that of Donald Williams.[33] At the outset of his work Williams claims that induction can be justified by analytic a priori means as a formal relation holding between propositions. In particular, the conclusion at which he wishes to arrive is the thesis that "knowledge that in an observed part of a class M the property P is present in a certain proportion gives us a *reason,* analogous to that provided by the premises of a syllogism though less conclusive, for believing that in the whole of the class M the property P is present in a similar proportion." The claim for "reason" (instead of "proof") and "analogy" (instead of "homology") is only the first dilution of Williams's theory. By the end of the work, in fact, much less is fulfilled than was initially promised. In his argument for

32. Niels Bohr, "On the Notions of Causality and Complementarity," *Dialectica,* 2 (1948): 312 ff.

33. D. Williams, *The Ground of Induction* (Cambridge, Mass.: Harvard University Press, 1947).

the propositional entailment of class statements by sample statements, Williams relies on the intermediacy of what is claimed to be "an analytic truism": namely, the law of large numbers. This is described as "an *a priori* law of classes, demonstrable by logical analysis."[34]

It is obvious from Williams's argument that he recognizes the need for some such mediating premise as the law of large numbers. The crucial question in evaluating his solution is whether that law, or any reasonable equivalent, is indeed an analytic truism or whether it is an arbitrary assumption postulating what it is required to support: namely, that there exists a logical bond between the relative frequency of a property in a sample population and the relative frequency of that property in the whole population. Certainly if such a logical bond obtains, it follows that inductive propositions—at least those that generalize from a sample—can be deduced. But it is precisely the logical character of this bond that Williams fails to establish. The law of large numbers itself, therefore, remains an inductive principle assumed for the purposes of justifying induction, and Hume's question still goes begging: "Where is the medium, the interposing ideas, which join propositions so very wide of each other?"[35]

What appears to be the most fruitful method of circumventing Hume's criticism is to treat inductive inference as the application of probability theory. Like the previous proposal, this one may also be examined by considering a sample argument in its favor.[36] Feigl criticizes Hume for treating the degree of probability in favor of an induction

34. *Ibid.*, pp. 20, 81, 139.
35. *Enquiry*, p. 37.
36. H. Feigl, "The Logical Character of the Principle of Induction," in *Readings in Philosophical Analysis* (New York: Appleton-Century-Crofts, 1949).

as a psychological or subjective matter, specifically as a degree of belief or an intensity of expectation based on habit. This is a fair summary of the view expressed in *Enquiry* VI. Against this, Feigl raises the possibility of two objective interpretations of induction: probability considered as a logical relation (after Leibniz, Bolzano, Nicod, Keynes) ; and probability considered as the limit of a statistical frequency (after Venn, Peirce, Mises) . The former is rejected for much the same reasons as those adduced against it by Russell[37] and Strawson:[38] namely, that it is an inductive justification of induction and therefore begs the question. Feigl's solution is to consider the probability of induction as the extrapolation of statistical frequencies not involving the predication of any probability at all:

> The principle of induction, formulated in terms of the frequency theory, states simply that those regularities which have held so far without exception will be found to hold most frequently in the future. According to this analysis, the probability of induction is always secondary and hypothetical, and can never be a genuine attribute of pure generalization.[39]

What seems to me most striking about this formulation of the frequency theory is that it is a paraphrase of Hume's formulation—with the difference that Feigl proffers a bare assertion without Hume's explanatory reference to psychological expectation. How this change suffices to render induction objective is not at all clear. Apparently Feigl also saw that the principle of induction could not be left in the form of an assertion, since it would then be open

37. B. Russell, *Human Knowledge: Its Scope and Limits* (New York: Simon and Schuster, 1948) , pt. 5.
38. P. F. Strawson, *Introduction to Logical Theory* (London: Methuen, 1952) , chapter 9.
39. Feigl, p. 301.

to the same demand for justification as any other inductive
assertion. He therefore proceeds to transmute his original
statement into something that will be immune to this
demand—"a hypothetical imperative" whose "meaning is
not factual but motivational." Thus the "real" principle
of induction is made to read as follows:

> Seek to achieve a maximum of order by logical operations
> upon elementary propositions. Generalize this order (what-
> ever its form be: causal, statistical or other), with a minimum
> or arbitrariness, that is, according to the principle of sim-
> plicity.[40]

This reformulation of the inductive principle—or, as it
now stands, procedure—does not seem to me either to save
it from sceptical questioning or to eliminate from it an
implicit psychological element. First, if the assertion is
vulnerable to the question "Why is it so?" the hypothetical
imperative is equally vulnerable to the question "Why
should I follow this procedure?" Second, the hypothetical
imperative can be taken as secondary to, or derived from,
the psychological description of how we in fact proceed
in inductive judgments. Considered in this light, Feigl's
hypothetical imperative is the counterpart of Wittgenstein's description:

> The procedure of induction consists in accepting as true the
> *simplest* law that can be reconciled with our experiences. This
> procedure, however, has no logical justification but only a
> psychological one.[41]

The nature of the psychological justification consists in
the fact, observed by Hume, that where a particular effect

---

40. *Ibid.*, pp. 302 f.
41. L. Wittgenstein, *Tractatus Logico-Philosophicus*, trans. Pears and
McGuinness (London: Routledge & Kegan Paul, 1961), pp. 6 and 363 f.

has always been found conjoined with a particular cause, we always expect the effect upon the appearance of the cause; and where several effects have been found to follow from a single cause, we proportion our expectation of the possible effects according to the quantitative experience of their conjunction with the cause.

In conclusion it is worth noting that, in the same way that the physical sciences have been found to be compatible with acausalism, probability theory has been found to be compatible with subjectivism. The apparent ineradicability of a subjective element in probability has led to its incorporation among the basic concepts of that science. Thus the Bayesian method considers probability to be concerned with "degrees of belief" which depend on three variables: the proposition believed, the proposition assumed, and "the general state of mind of the person who is doing the believing."[42] "Belief" itself is taken as a primitive notion and, although Bayesian probability is not thereby rendered a less rigorous system, it does explicitly admit to using as its raw material "subjective judgements . . . [without which] the theory would be tautological in the sense in which pure mathematics is tautological."[43] This concession to subjectivity is necessitated by the fact that, without arbitrary stipulation, there simply does not exist a sample of samples. Consequently, in estimating the probability of a binomial distribution the Bayesian must either guess the distribution of one element "or he must select [it] to 'represent his ignorance.' "[44]

42. I. J. Good, *Probability and the Weighing of Evidence* (London: Charles Griffin, 1950), chapter 1.

43. *Ibid.*, preface.

44. I. J. Good, *The Estimation of Probabilities* (Cambridge, Mass.: M. I. T. Press, 1965, pp. 7 ff. Cf. also H. Jeffreys, *Theory of Probability*, 3rd. ed. (Oxford: Clarendon Press, 1961), chapter 1.

Abstract Reason and Value Judgments

The two concomitant doctrines we have so far examined, the limitation of abstract reason to relations of ideas and the inapplicability of abstract reason to matters of fact, were undoubtedly among the most important and novel aspects of Hume's mental geography. The relation of abstract reason to irrational cognition, if not strictly entailed by these doctrines, is at least implicit in them. In his arguments for the nondeducibility of ethical and theological propositions, Hume was able to rely to some extent on the work of the moral-sense philosophers and the proponents of natural religion respectively. Therefore, the *Enquiry* is able to dispense with lengthy arguments on these subjects.

Hume considers ethical and, in general, evaluative questions to be concerned with "principles which . . . excite our sentiments, and make us approve or blame any particular object, action, or behaviour," and the rationalist approach to the same questions as the quest "for some common principle, on which this variety of sentiments might depend." However, while Hume's principle is descriptive, what he attributes to the rationalists is the desire to establish principles that express "eternal and immutable relations, which to every intelligent mind are equally invariable as any proposition concerning quantity or number."[45]

The rebuttal of a deductivist ethic is contained in *Treatise* III and in the second *Enquiry*. In the first *Enquiry* Hume does not offer any detailed counter-argument to it. He is more concerned with dissociating ethics from

---

45. *Enquiry*, pp. 6 and 15. See also the second edition of the *Enquiry*, ed. E. C. Mossner (New York: Washington Square Press, 1963) , p. 18 n.

experimental reason and from theological arguments. However, it follows both from his analysis of the scope of abstract reason and from his definition of the nature of ethics that the latter does not come within the province of the former. If reason impinges in any way at all on the sphere of ethics, and Hume suggests that it does, then it is only insofar as ethics is concerned with judgments on states of affairs; and hence the only rational faculty that might come into play with regard to ethical propositions is experimental reason.

Abstract Reason and Theology

It was true of Hume's day, the era of the deist controversy, that "there is not a greater number of philosophical reasonings, displayed upon any subject, than those, which prove the existence of a Deity, and refute the fallacies of Atheists." What Hume has called the religious hypothesis consists, in his view, of one primary and several secondary elements. The former is the assertion that God exists; the latter is the predication to this real existence of various attributes, volitions, and activities. In Hume's terms, the main elements of the hypothesis are judgments concerning "a divine existence, and consequently a divine providence and a future state." The religious hypothesis suggests that God is the creator and the "supreme governor of the world, who guides the course of events, and punishes the vicious with infamy and disappointment, and rewards the virtuous with honour and success."[46]

Hume has a dual epistemological interest in the hypothesis: first, to ascertain how we can possibly know the

---

46. *Enquiry*, pp. 133 f., 149.

hypothesis itself; and second, whether (given the hypothesis) any other facts or propositions can be derived from it. For the present, I shall limit discussion to the first of these aspects, and in particular to the relevance of abstract reason to the proof or disproof of the hypothesis.

Hume does not consider in detail what passed among his contemporaries and predecessors as a priori arguments in favor of the religious hypothesis. These arguments generally took one of two forms: arguments for the necessary existence of God (the ontological argument, the argument from degrees of perfection, and the argument from contingency and necessity) , and various forms of the causal argument (the cosmological argument and the prime-mover argument) . He neither affirms nor denies the efficacy of these arguments: he simply denies that they are a priori.

> That the divinity may *possibly* be endowed with attributes, which we have never seen exerted; may be governed by principles of action, which we cannot discover to be satisfied: all this will be freely allowed. But still this is mere *possibility* and hypothesis. We never can have reason to *infer* any attributes, or any principles of action in him, but so far as we know them to have been exerted and satisfied.
> Not only the will of the supreme Being may create matter; but, for aught we know *a priori,* the will of any other being might create it, or any other cause, that the most whimsical imagination can assign.[47]

Since the religious hypothesis consists of affirmations regarding real existences and matters of fact, and since both kinds of affirmation are calculable solely by experimental reason, it follows that if the religious hypothesis is to be judged by any form of reason, then it is to be judged by experimental reason. And indeed it is to the empirical

47. *Ibid.*, pp. 141 and 164.

arguments for the existence of God that Hume addresses himself in some detail in the *Enquiry*. Abstract reason is indifferent to the hypothesis.

Hume's theory of abstract reason, then, may be summed up as the claim that whatever knowledge can be derived by abstract reason is derived by the application of abstract reason to its proper cognitive sphere—relations of ideas—and that the misapplication of abstract reason to other cognitive spheres—matters of fact, value judgments, and the religious hypothesis—produces at best inconclusive results.

5

Experimental Reason

Experimental Reason and Matters of Fact

Reason, according to Hume, is the exercise of calculative procedures on given conceptual or perceptual material. Certain kinds of argument, those governed by the law of contradiction, are amenable to the procedures of abstract reason. However, other species of human calculation are not so governed and are therefore not amenable to analytic procedures. How these nonanalytic arguments are calculable is the subject of Hume's investigation into experimental reason.

Hume takes the objects of experimental reason to be matters of fact: that is, what is expressible by factual or existential propositions (or propositions that do not infringe the law of contradiction) —other than those with a perceptual or an evaluative or a theological content. Loosely, this defines what today would be termed elliptic or explicit inductive inferences. His reduction of the question of how such inferences are justified to the question of how we can know causal laws is perhaps the only undisputed aspect of his theory of experimental reason. It is his treatment of the nature and our knowledge of causal laws and the supposed implications of Hume's solution to these questions that have formed the background to the controversy over Hume's theory.

Formulated as a law, causality makes it possible, given certain factual or existential factors, to infer something about other factual or existential factors. It assumes that the unobserved parameters in, say, an experimental situation possess precise values which, if they were known, would make precise prediction of the experiment possible so long as the known parameters remain constant. Thus, if an exclusive causal relation is said to hold between two events, A and B, it is possible from the observation of either A or B to infer the past or future or simultaneous occurrence of the absent member of the pair.

Hume explicitly deals with the predictive and the "retrodictive" utility of causality. As an instance of the former he cites the predictive inference that bodily contact with fire will prove painful; of the latter, the inference regarding the existence of past human habitation in a presently uninhabited locality where there are ruins and other human artifacts.[1] To these might be added the importance of causal laws in inferring concurrent events, as when doctors use visible symptoms to infer the presence of disease germs. What is common to these otherwise

1. The *Enquiry* abounds in paradigms of experimental reason. See D. Hume, *Enquiries concerning the Human Understanding and the Principles of Morals*, ed. L. A. Selby-Bigge, 2nd ed. (Oxford: Oxford University Press, 1902), pp. 26, 29, 33, 43, 45, 51, 56, 58, 63, 66, 69, 77, 84, 87, 91, 98, among others.

diverse instances is that the inference proceeds from something known (given in sense experience or memory) to something unknown. The link between the present fact and that which is inferred from it is the supposition that they are causally connected, and that such an inference is therefore possible.

The negative part of Hume's analysis of the concept of causality consists of the argument that certain of the faculties are incapable of acting as the cognitive source of the notion of causality. The positive part of his doctrine consists of what claims to be a description of how the causal link is actually discovered. In his quest for the proper source of this notion, Hume takes as the basis of his further argument two empirical observations.

The first of these is the claim that a causal relation is known to obtain among events or things only after appropriate experience of one of three types. One of these may be called the repeated homologous experience:

> It is only after a long course of uniform experiments in any kind, that we attain a firm reliance and security with regard to a particular event. . . . When one particular species of event has always, in all instances, been conjoined with another, we make no longer any scruple of foretelling one upon the appearance of the other, and of employing that reasoning, which can alone assure us of any matter of fact or existence. We then call the one object, *Cause;* the other, *Effect.*[2]

Another is the repeated analogous experience:

> Where the causes are entirely similar, the analogy is perfect [that is, homologous], and the inference, drawn from it, is regarded as certain and conclusive. . . . But where the objects have not so exact a similarity, the analogy is less perfect, and the inference is less conclusive; though still it has some force, in proportion to the degree of similarity and resemblance. . . .

2. *Ibid.,* pp. 36 and 74 f.

When the circulation of the blood, for instance, is clearly proved [by homologous experience] to have place in one creature, as a frog, or fish, it forms a strong presumption [by analogy], that the same principle has place in all.[3]

And a third is the traumatic experience:

When a child has felt the sensation of pain from touching the flame of a candle, he will be careful not to put his hand near any candle, but will expect a similar effect from a cause which is similar in its sensible qualities and appearance.[4]

Of these three, the first two are the most typical and, therefore, the most important. In general, it is only after repeated instances of homologous or analogous experiences that the idea of a causal link obtaining among events arises.

Hume's second basic observation relies on a view which in philosophy has had a revival of popularity since 1953. It is that what we mean by experimental reasoning is reflected by, and can be observed in, the actions consequent on this species of reasoning. By this standard, we may be said to engage in behavior indicative of at least implicit reliance on the efficacy of causal laws—if not always of conscious experimental calculus—when we eat bread in the expectation that it will nourish us, when we shoot one billiard ball at another in the expectation that the second will be deflected at an angle in a desired direction, when we light a fire in the expectation of warmth, or when we draw a bow over a violin string in the expectation of producing a certain sound (all examples drawn from the *Enquiry*). Apparently similar behavior and, therefore, apparently similarly motivated behavior is discernible in children and in animals.

3. *Ibid.*, p. 104.
4. *Ibid.*, p. 39.

Coupled with this, and connecting it with his reflections on the need for repeated experience of causal conjunctions, is the observation that such behavior tends to improve in proportion to the increase in the number of relevant experiences: the more experience we have of causal conjunctions, the more confident our manipulation of materials and events.

In his analysis of abstract reason, Hume had sought the original principle of that cognitive activity outside of abstract reason itself, and he had found it in intuition and demonstration. In the case of experimental reason, he argues that to justify inductive inference by assuming a causal axiom (or some equivalent notion), or to justify causality by assuming the validity of the inferences based upon it, would beg the question.[5] He therefore relies on his two observations to provide the clue as to the nature and origin of experimental reason. From his first observation he concludes that the reasoning itself is something in the nature of what today would be termed a conditioned reflex; from the second he concludes that the practice of cause-governed or motivated behavior is, at least at a fundamental level, an unintellectualized involuntary response:

> Experimental reasoning itself, which we possess in common with beasts, and on which the whole conduct of life depends, is nothing but a species of instinct or mechanical power, that acts in us unknown to ourselves; and in its chief operations, is not directed by any such relations or comparisons of ideas, as are the proper objects of our intellectual faculties. Though the instinct be different, yet still it is an instinct, which teaches a man to avoid the fire; as much as that, which teaches a bird, with such exactness, the art of incubation, and the whole economy and order of its nursery.[6]

5. *Ibid.*, pp. 35 f.
6. *Ibid.* p. 108.

The mental counterpart of the instinctiveness of conditioned behavior is the "custom or habit" whereby, in the presence of one of a pair of causally related events or objects, the mind is conveyed to the idea of the absent member of the pair.[7] This habit is expressed in the "belief" that, where the cause is observed to have occurred, the effect is assumed to follow or to have followed; and that, where the effect is observed to have occurred, the occurrence of the cause is assumed. In either case, the degree of certainty attaching to the belief is conditioned by the past numerical instantiation of the causal conjunction under consideration. Stated in general terms, Hume's doctrine amounts to the claim that the habitual transition of the mind from present cause to absent effect (or vice versa) results in an involuntary belief in the efficacy of causes proportionate to the quantitative experience of the relevant conjunctions in the past. This belief—like the action consequent upon it—is "a species of natural instinct, which no reasoning or process of the thought and understanding is able either to produce or to prevent."[8]

There is one feature of Hume's analysis of causality that is determined by his theory of meaning (see next chapter). In this theory he claims it to be requisite for a term to have meaning that it shall ultimately be traceable to an "impression." Having reduced the notion of causality to a mode of behavior reflecting a belief, Hume attaches meaning to the initial term in his series by attributing to the final term the character of a particular species of impression: namely, a "feeling or inward sentiment" denoted by the term *belief*. Beyond asserting that belief is not an independent sentiment or impression, but

7. *Ibid.*, pp. 43, 55, 58, 69.
8. *Ibid.*, pp. 46 f., 56 f., 75, 106.

rather that it is attached as a qualitative modifier to exist-
ing impressions, Hume abandons the attempt to define
belief itself. He is content (like I. J. Good, chapter 4
above) to let it stand as a primitive term. An interesting
feature of Hume's theory of belief is the barely developed
suggestion that action consequent on belief may be taken
as a criterion of belief: presumably, I may be said to
believe that there is a step before me in the dark when
I make the appropriate movement in anticipation of
mounting it.[9]

So far, Hume's reductive analysis of experimental reasoning has proceeded in two stages. First, he has reduced
every instance of inductive inference to an instance of
causal reasoning, or reasoning in which the causal principle is the fundamental assumption. Second, he has
reduced the causal principle itself to its basic components.
In the case of causal reasoning considered as a practice,
the basic component is instinctive adaptation; considered
as a theory, it is instinctive belief. Hume attempts to
justify each of these reductive analyses by, among other
means, arguing the untenability of its contrary. In support
of the first, he instances typical inductive inferences which
he can show rely on the principle of causality. He then
assumes the right to postulate that *all* similar inferences
rely on that principle unless and until an exceptional
instance can be cited. In support of the second, his method
is to eliminate all other faculties as possible sources for
the cognition of causality.[10]

The analysis of causality might lead one reasonably to
anticipate a definition of that concept in terms of the ele-

---

9. *Ibid.*, pp. 47 f. and 49 f.
10. See for example *Enquiry*, pp. 27, 31, 38, and 70 f. for arguments
respectively against perceptual, abstract, experimental, and divine origins
of causal cognition.

ments to which it has been reduced. In fact, Hume offers three distinct definitions:

> We may define a cause to be *an object, followed by another, and where all the objects similar to the first are followed by objects similar to the second.* Or in other words *where, if the first object had not been, the second never had existed. . . .* We may . . . form another definition of cause, and call it, *an object followed by another, and whose appearance always conveys the thought to that other.*[11]

Hume's definition or definitions of cause constitute an instance of verbal legerdemain the extent of which seems to have eluded all but a few commentators.[12] By interposing "or in other words" between his first two definitions, Hume claims that they are logically equivalent, a claim which cannot in fact be demonstrated: the first definition is sequential and the second necessitarian. He also claims that some sort of relation—the precise nature of which remains ambiguous—obtains between the first two and the third, while in fact, the third definition is psychological. There are four subsequent reiterations of the definitions of cause.[13] In all of these the first two are consolidated so that only the sequential definition remains. This is then presented either conjunctively or disjunctively with the psychological definition: in the first two and in the last, they are reiterated conjunctively; in the third, disjunctively. The nature of the relation between the two remaining definitions is not clarified by Hume's enigmatic rider to the effect that the sequential and the psychological definitions "are at bottom the same."[14]

---

11. *Ibid.,* pp. 76 f.
12. Credit for spotting the nonequivalence of the first two definitions must go to Selby-Bigge (see his introduction to the *Enquiries,* p. xviii).
13. *Enquiry,* pp. 92 (twice), 97, 159.
14. *Ibid.,* p. 97.

Critique of Hume's Theory of Experimental Reason and Matters of Fact

Because Hume insists on the presence of an impression as the condition for the meaningfulness of a term, and because the appropriate impression is a psychological product of phenomenal sequentiality, I consider it likely that Hume intends the conjunction (rather than the disjunction) of his definitions to provide the analysis of cause. In any case, it is clear that he intends it to be through some function or other of these definitions that we are led to "infer the existence of one object from the appearance of the other" or "one event from the other."[15] This raises the question of whether even the two definitions taken jointly exhaust what we mean when we use the term *cause* in the sense of one event, A, causing another event, B. There remains the suspicion that Hume's definitions omit something essential to cause beyond the frequently observed sequence of events that are homologous (or analogous) to A and B, and the consequent evocation, on observing another instance of A, of a mental anticipation of B.

One simple solution would be to assert that what has been omitted is something belonging to the causally related elements A and B, rather than something pertaining to the mind of the observer. Such a solution would, however, still run into the same difficulties that led to Hume's psychological formulation in the first place. It would have to identify precisely what that something is; and, assuming that the missing element can be identified, it would have to enucleate the cognitive process whereby this ele-

15. *Ibid.*, pp. 42, 79.

ment can be known. From his consideration of such concepts as "power," "force," "energy," "*vis inertiae*," and "necessary connexion," Hume concludes that they are either synonymous with all or part of what is meant by cause or "without meaning"[16]—untraceable to any impression.

Apart from Hume's arguments in favor of his theory, it is also possible to hold on linguistic grounds that the two definitions are sufficient determinants for the concept of causality. Suppose there were no such thing as a conjunction, such that there obtained between its elements an objective causal bond, and there were only such conjunctions as those described by Hume. There would thus be a type of conjunction in which events homologous (or analogous) with event A were frequently observed to be spatially and temporally sequent on events homologous (or analogous) with event B, and such that on the appearance of one we anticipated the occurrence of the other. This type of conjunction would need to be differentiated in language from other conjunctions which, while equally sequential, were not associated with frequent observation or with a feeling of anticipation.

Empirically, the two types of conjunction would be characterized respectively by the presence and the absence of the frequency element; psychologically, by the presence and the absence of the anticipatory element; and epistemologically, by the presence and the absence of inductive inferences consequent on the observation of one member of the conjunctive pair. If these differences are linguistically denoted, the term assigned to the first type of conjunction will, in use, be indistinguishable from what in natural languages is termed "causal conjunction"; and

16. *Ibid.*, pp. 62, 72 f., 96.

that assigned to the second, indistinguishable from "casual conjunction." Hence it seems that Hume's sequential and psychological definitions taken jointly are sufficient for the correct application of the term "cause" in natural languages even if an essential element is omitted.

The view that Hume's definition dissolves the concept of causality rather than analyzes it arises from a misunderstanding of his intention. The reality (objectivity) or otherwise of causality is not at issue. In fact, Hume takes a rather naïve view of this question and he postulates a theory—reminiscent of the Cartesian explanation for the parallelism of material and spiritual motions—to account for the harmony between the operation of causes in nature and the concept of causality as an associative principle among ideas.[17] Neither is Hume particularly interested in the meaning of causality or in the correct application of causal locutions. The focus of his interest is the epistemological question regarding the origin and nature of our *knowledge* of causes, the concept itself being given. In the case of cause, as in the case of the self and material objects and other entities regarding which he is alleged to have reached sceptical conclusions, he does not ask "What *is* so and so?" nor does he ask "What do we *mean* by so and so?": rather he asks "How do we *know* so and so?"

In addressing himself to the analysis of causality in the *Enquiry,* his formulation of the problem is this:

> It is universally allowed that matter, in all its operations, is actuated by a necessary force, and that every natural effect is so precisely determined by the energy of its cause that no other effect, in such particular circumstances, could possibly have resulted from it. . . . Would we, therefore, form a just and precise idea of *necessity,* we must consider whence that idea arises when we apply it to the operation of bodies.[18]

17. *Ibid.,* pp. 50, 54.
18. *Ibid.,* p. 82.

There does not appear to be a logical incompatibility between the assumption that there exist objective causes and a psychological description of how we know causes any more, say, than there is between the assertions "Joe lives in Jerusalem" and "All I know of Joe is by hearsay."

Let us turn now to another criticism of Hume's theory of experimental reason. For it is not only on the ground of its allegedly incomplete analysis of the concept with which it deals that it has been attacked. It seems to be the view that his interpretation of causality entails the conclusion either that inference is always and necessarily irrational; or that it cannot be established whether there exists a rational inference, since his analysis leaves no room for distinguishing correct from incorrect inferences.[19]

If this is the consequence of Hume's theory of experimental reason, then to the extent that Hume's theory is true, it argues against the rationality of induction or against the possibility of establishing criteria for the correctness of inductive inferences. But it does not follow from the fact that the consequences of the theory are repugnant that the theory is wrong. Even if it did follow, however, the choice between accepting the repugnant consequences and rejecting the theory would not need to be made, I believe, since the repugnant consequences are not in fact entailed when all the ramifications of the theory are considered.

It is true that Hume takes the basis of experimental

---

19. See for example H. Reichenbach, "A Conversation between Bertrand Russell and David Hume," *Journal of Philosophy*, 46 (1949) : pp. 546 f.; A. E. Taylor, *Philosophical Studies* (London: Macmillan, 1934) , pp. 353 ff.; D. S. Miller, "Hume's Deathblow to Deductivism," *Journal of Philosophy*, 46 (1949) : 745; H. A. Prichard, *Knowledge and Perception* (Oxford: Oxford University Press, 1950) , p. 177; A. Flew, *Hume's Philosophy of Belief* (London: Routledge and Kegan Paul, 1961) , pp. 87–92; and J. A. Passmore, *Hume's Intentions* (Cambridge: Cambridge University Press, 1952) , p. 64.

reason to be a concept whose origin is not rational. In this
he says no more than does a more recent philosopher in
discussing the same question:

> As a practice, induction is nothing but our old friend, the
> law of conditioned reflexes or of association. A child touches
> a knob that gives him an electric shock; after that, he avoids
> touching the knob. If he is old enough to speak, he may state
> that the knob hurts when it is touched; he has made an in-
> duction based on a single instance. But the induction will
> exist as a bodily habit even if he is too young to speak, and it
> occurs equally among animals, provided they are not too low
> in the scale.[20]

For Hume as well as for Russell, animal inference is
only the starting point of intellectual induction. Those
passages in the *Enquiry* that are often cited as evidence
that Hume holds all induction to be irrational refer, as
the context indicates, to the primitive inferential activity
that Russell calls the practice of induction. Rational induction too has its roots in the same phenomena as animal
induction: for Hume these phenomena are sequentiality
and the psychological state of the observer. However,
unlike the conditioned animal or the burnt child, rational
man is able to transcend his instinctive responses and to
dispense with exclusive reliance on his inward sentiment
for the cognition of causes. This development is achieved
by generalizing, or rationalizing, the practice of animal
induction into the rules of probability calculus. The consistent application of these rules is the exercise of experimental reason.[21] And it is none the less a rational activity
—that is, the application of a calculus—for following a
pattern established as a conditioned response. Once the

---

20. B. Russell, *An Outline of Philosophy* (London: Allen and Unwin,
1932) , pp. 83 f.
21. For paradigms of such rationalizations see *Enquiry* VI.

generalization is achieved and the calculus systematized, the need for direct observation disappears. What was an instinctive reaction becomes a rational activity. We can calculate the chances of a crap game mathematically without going near a game; and the same calculation will persuade a rational man not to bet on these chances even before he has lost a cent.[22]

It is the calculable element in inductive inference that justifies Hume in counting the activity as rational and the faculty as reason. In so designating experimental reason, Hume classes it with abstract reason and distinguishes both from the irrational faculties. The latter are characterized not only by not needing an intermediary calculus between premises and conclusion, but by such a calculus being considered in such cases as either irrelevant or as the source of philosophic error. No calculus, for example, is needed to inform me that I have a toothache. It is not relevant to the validity of Hume's theory that a calculus is required to locate the source of the toothache, or that what I take to be a toothache may really be hysterical pain. Both kinds of identification difficulty are a function of the systematically misleading nature of the expression used in verbalizing sense experience. The point of the distinction is that "toothache"—whether or not it is correctly designated—represents a class of direct apprehensions in which there is no series from premises to conclusion.

Since experimental reason involves the application of a calculus, there exists a criterion of correctness in the application of the calculus; and since the calculus is founded on previous experience, there exists a criterion

22. If he still bets on a crap game, it is either because he has crooked dice or because he hopes *against* the evidence to bring off a win.

for the correctness of the formulation of the calculus. The
calculus will be correctly formulated if it truly describes
the frequency with which the parameters of an experiment have been associated; and it will be correctly applied if the association is consistently projected for
predictive purposes according to experienced regularities.
The degree of accuracy with which these mathematical
procedures are effected constitutes Hume's standard of
just reasoning.[23] Hence, although it rests on a psychological foundation, what is accepted as a correct inference
can after all be rationally distinguished from guessing or
from superstition.

In formulating the criteria and the rules of just reasoning, Hume does not claim to be providing absolute
standards. What he does claim to do is to describe what
in fact occurs when we are said to make a reasonable
inductive inference:

> A wise man . . . proportions his belief to the evidence. In
> such conclusions as are founded on an infallible experience, he
> expects the event with the last degree of assurance, and regards
> his past experience as a full *proof* of the future existence of
> that event. In other cases, he proceeds with more caution: He
> weighs the opposite experiments: He considers which side is
> supported by the greater number of experiments: to that side
> he inclines, with doubt and hesitation; and when at last he
> fixes his judgement, the evidence exceeds not what we prop-
> erly call *probability*.[24]

It is the fact of residual credence which, for Hume, justifies the rule of residual probability:

> In all cases, we must balance the opposite experiments, where
> they are opposite, and deduct the smaller number from the

23. On "just reasoning," see *Enquiry*, pp. 58, 85, 105, 107, 110 f., 113,
114 ff., 124, 127, 130, 136, 139 ff., 141.
24. *Ibid.*, p. 110 f.

greater, in order to know the exact force of the superior evidence.[25]

Similarly, the fact that we expect effects to be commensurate with causes permits us to formulate what we may call the rule of causal commensurability:

> When we infer any particular cause from an effect, we must proportion the one to the other, and can never be allowed to ascribe to the cause any qualities, but what are exactly sufficient to produce the effect.[26]

The principal argument in favor of these rules is not the pragmatic one that adherence to these rules leads, by and large, to correct predictions: Hume considers the procedure correct even when it leads to false conclusions.[27] His argument is, rather, that if we abandon the psychologically based rules of inference for some "chimerical" absolute standard, "we are got into fairy land, long ere we have reached the last steps of our theory."[28]

Before leaving Hume's positive theory of experimental reason, at least bare mention must be made of two remaining problems. The first of these concerns the reciprocal relation between phenomenal conjunctions and mental expectation.[29] Hume apparently takes it that the former somehow cause the latter. He thereby assumes the operation of causality even in his own analysis of that concept. But the assumption is operational rather than philosophical. That is, he assumes the relationship merely as a guess as to why we think in causal terms, not to explain the mode of causal thought itself. The second concerns

25. *Ibid.*, p. 111.
26. *Ibid.*, p. 136.
27. *Ibid.*, pp. 113 f.
28. *Ibid.*, p. 72.
29. This is discussed in Passmore, pp. 75 ff.

Hume's theory of just reasoning. Here he commits what may be called the Euthyphro Fallacy (after Plato's dialogue of that name) of defining just reasoning as being what just reasoners practice. It remains to be seen whether these difficulties are intractable or whether they can be dissolved by reformulating Hume's questions, or his answers, or both.

Experimental Reason and Value Judgments

In discussing the misapplication of experimental reason, Hume addressed himself in particular to instances of this in relation to perception and theology. It was the misuse of experimental reason in these spheres that was most common and that led to what he considered the most insidious errors. On the other hand, while argument was required to combat the extension of deductivity to matters of fact, there were few instances or none of the misapplication of experimental reason to the abstract sphere. Deductive knowledge was in any case regarded as the only appropriate approach to the abstract sciences.

Although ethical and aesthetic propositions constitute a distinct class within Hume's system, he does not consider value judgments to be entirely unamenable to experimental calculation. Hume accounts for this by postulating a theory similar to that regarding the harmony that is supposed to obtain between our causal notions and natural operations. In the case of ethics, there is observed to be a more than occasional, but less than complete, coincidence between what engages our approbation and what is empirically known to be socially useful. There is a like coincidence between what arouses opprobrium and what is socially harmful. Again, there is observed to be a coincidence between the judgments of the moral sense and what is generally approved and disapproved among mankind.[30] Hence, although ethical judgments proper are directly apprehended and are therefore incalculable, experimental reason may be applied to the empirical judgments that generally concur with them. In such cases, however, the conclusions of experimental reason are not strictly about ethical matters, but rather about "a new fact, to wit, the general tastes of mankind, or some such fact, which may be the object of reasoning and enquiry."[31]

Experimental Reason and Percepts

The relation between experimental reason and perception is limited to the inferential distinction between veridical and illusory appearances. That is, experimental reason can, on the basis of comparison with previous experience, establish with some probability what form appearances would take under normal conditions when the present appearance deviates from the norm because of some special circumstance attending the perception.[32] The terms "veridical" and "illusory" in this context must be understood in a relative or subjective sense, as the inference relates to the appearance and not to some independent event or object to which the appearance can be related.

This leads to the question of whether we can infer from sense experience the existence of such objects—external bodies, or an external world, or real entities, as they have

30. *Enquiry*, pp. 102 and 165.
31. *Ibid.*, p. 165.
32. *Ibid.*, p. 151.

been variously called. It would seem that if such objects can be inferred at all then it is by means of experimental reason that they are inferred, and that if they are to be inferred from anything then it is from percepts that the inference is made. Almost the entire literature on Hume is agreed that his negative doctrines on the subject suggest that he favors the latter position in what is known as the realist-idealist controversy. Differences of opinion among the commentators concern mainly the question of what precise form of phenomenalism, monism, or nominalism he adopts in defining his idealist position. Some such interpretation would be correct, but only if it is presupposed that idealism is the only alternative to realism. However, while it is true that in the *Enquiry* Hume attacks both varieties of realist theory then current, it does not in fact follow from his rejection of these theories that he was an idealist. Hume actually adopted another alternative: the inapplicability of experimental reason to the problem.

The realism that Hume attacked was the supposition that a material body "preserves its existence uniform and entire, independent of the situation of intelligent beings, who perceive or contemplate it."[33] This much is common to both varieties of realism—naïve (or direct) realism and the representative theory of perception. Hume's objections to the former are discussed in chapter 6 below. The representative theory of perception as defined by Hume consists in the belief or the assumption that "perceptions in the mind [are] fleeting copies or representations of

---

33. *Ibid.*, p. 152. Compare this with W. T. Stace, who defines realism as a doctrine maintaining that "some entities sometimes exist without being experienced by any finite mind" ("The Refutation of Realism," reprinted in *A Modern Introduction to Philosophy*, ed. Edwards and Pap (New York: Free Press of Glencoe, 1962), p. 199.

other existences, which remain uniform and independent." The usual way of accounting for the mechanism of representation is causal: "that the perceptions of the mind must be caused by external objects, entirely different from them, though resembling them."[34] A causal association is, however, not essential to the theory; what is essential is the claim that there are two classes of cognitive object, the first of these known by acquaintance[35] and the other inferred from these. Thus the representative theory of perception proceeds on the assumption that material objects, the inferred entities, can always and only be known mediately. But if this is the case, then it is impossible—in Hume's sense of the term—that they could ever be inferred at all; for it is an indispensable condition of inference that the inferred entity or something analogous to it shall have been previously experienced in association with that from which it is inferred.

Hume's conclusion from this argument is that though the question of the reality of material bodies seems to be an existential question and therefore one that is subject to experimental reason,

> . . . here experience is, and must be entirely silent. The mind
> has never anything present to it but the perceptions, and can-
> not possibly reach any experience of their connexion with
> objects. The supposition of such a connexion is, therefore,
> without any foundation in reasoning.[36]

---

34. *Enquiry*, p. 152.
35. Roughly in the sense given to this expression by Russell in "Knowledge by Acquaintance and Knowledge by Description," *Proceedings of the Aristotelian Society*, 11 (1910–11).
36. *Enquiry*, 153. Stace, expresses in modern terms much of the substance of Hume's argument and his conclusions. For differing views, see A. M. Quinton, "The Problem of Perception", *Mind*, 64 (1955); C. D. Broad, "Some Elementary Reflexions on Sense-Perception," *Philosophy*, 27 (1952); and D. M. Armstrong, *Perception and the Physical World*, (London: Routledge and Kegan Paul, 1961), chapter 33.

While this is a conclusion that rejects realism, it is not one that accepts idealism: it concludes simply that experimental reason is inapplicable to the question. So far as Hume is concerned, the trouble with realism—and the same goes for idealism, *mutatis mutandis*—is not that it is false, but that it makes positive assertions concerning a matter about which, on the basis of experimental reason, no positive assertion can be made.

Experimental Reason and Theology

Of the various arguments for the religious hypothesis, the one that most readily lends itself to experimental reasoning seems to be the argument from design.[37] Indeed in claiming to be a proof of God's existence, the primary element of the hypothesis, it explicitly appeals to inductive inferences based on analogy; it does not claim either that direct acquaintance with God is possible or that experience of a homologous kind with the creation or the continued sustenance of the universe is possible. It is, therefore, weakened at the outset as an experimental argument by having to rely on a kind of argument with a relatively low degree of probability.

In the form that Hume discusses the argument from design, the analogy to the creation of the universe is drawn from human artifacts, whose complex and well-coordinated arrangement proves that they must have had an artificer whose purposeful creation they are. This can be inferred even if we are unacquainted with the artificer or were absent during the act of artifaction. An even more "glorious display of intelligence" than may be inferred

---

37. See A. Flew, *God and Philosophy* (London: Hutchinson, 1966), chapter 3.

from human artifacts is provided by "the order, beauty, and wise arrangement of the universe";[30] hence we may infer that the universe is the creation of a proportionately greater artificer—God.

The cogency of this as of any other argument from analogy depends on the degree of resemblance between the inferred case and its observed analogue. In the *Enquiry,* Hume confines himself to criticizing the analogy on the grounds of a numerical distinction. We have observed the conjunction between human artifact and artificer often enough for the second to be inferred from the first; but the universe is a unique production whose like we have never been able to observe in conjunction with its supposed maker. This makes the analogy so remote that "the religious hypothesis . . . must be considered only as a particular method of accounting for the visible phenomena of the universe."[39]

If experimental reason is able to infer, as one among other remote possibilities, the existence of God (or gods) from the order of the universe, it proves entirely incapable of inferring that this Designer has any of the additional attributes predicated of God in the religious hypothesis, or orthodox varieties of the hypothesis, current in Hume's day. Among these attributes, Hume places the alleged continuing benevolent intervention of God in the affairs of his creation and the dispensation of redress for both virtue and vice in the form of post-mortem reward and punishment. In the language of the time, these secondary postulates were "a particular providence" and "a future state."

Hume contends that neither of these could justly be

_____

38. *Enquiry,* p. 135.
39. *Ibid.,* p. 139.

inferred from the state of the universe. The effort to do so infringes the rule of just reasoning, which requires that the inferred cause be proportioned to the observed effect. In attributing to the Designer of the universe perfect intelligence and goodness, "infinite perfection" that "can intend nothing but what is altogether good and laudable," or a "divine providence" and "a supreme distributive justice,"[40] theologians attribute more to the cause than is evident in the effect:

> Allowing, therefore, the gods to be the authors of the existence or order of the universe; it follows, that they possess that precise degree of power, intelligence, and benevolence, which appears in their workmanship. . . . So far as the traces of any attributes, at present, appear, so far may we conclude these attributes to exist. . . . We can never be allowed to mount up from the universe, the effect, to Jupiter, the cause; and then descend downwards, to infer any new effect from that cause. . . . The knowledge of the cause being derived solely from the effect, they must be exactly adjusted to each other. . . . You persist in imagining, that, if we grant that divine existence, for which you so earnestly contend, you may safely infer consequences from it, and add something to the experienced order of nature, by arguing from the attributes which you ascribe to your gods. You seem not to remember, that all your reasonings on this subject can only be drawn from effects to causes; and that every argument, deducted from causes to effects, must of necessity be a gross sophism; since it is impossible for you to know anything of the cause, but what you have antecedently, not inferred, but discovered to the full, in the effect.[41]

Hume's criticism of the teleological argument in the *Enquiry* hinges on the closeness or remoteness of the analogy between an artifact and the universe. If the analogy is closer than he will allow, the precise proportioning of cause to effect is not necessary:

40. *Ibid.*, pp. 19, 100 f., 140.
41. *Ibid.*, pp. 137 and 140.

If you saw, for instance, a half-finished building, surrounded with heaps of brick and stone and mortar, and all the instruments of masonry; could you not *infer* from the effect, that it was a work of design and contrivance? And could you not return again, from this inferred cause, to infer new additions to the effect, and conclude, that the building would soon be finished, and receive all the further improvements, which art could bestow upon it?[42]

In the *Dialogues,* insistence on the proximity of the analogy is condemned as anthropocentric. In the *Enquiry,* the emphasis in his rebuttal is on the uniqueness of the universe:

The Deity is known to us only by his productions, and is a single being in the universe, not comprehended under any species or genus, from whose experienced attributes or qualities, we can, by analogy, infer any attribute or quality in him.[43]

Discounting other inherent defects of the teleological argument—discussion of which is confined to the *Dialogues* —what is needed to support Hume's disquisition on the subject in the *Enquiry* is a criterion of resemblance or degree of analogousness. In applying his own unstated criterion, Hume concludes that the resources of experimental reason are exhausted when, from the observed state of the universe, we infer "a Being, so remote and incomprehensible, who bears much less analogy to any other being in the universe than the sun to a waxen taper, and who discovers himself only by some faint traces or outlines, beyond which we have no authority to ascribe to him any attribute or perfection." Consequently, beyond the possible conclusion that the universe has a designer, "no new fact can ever be inferred from the religious hy-

42. *Ibid.,* pp. 142 f.
43. *Ibid.,* 144.

pothesis; no event foreseen or foretold; no reward or punishment expected or dreaded, beyond what is already known by practice and observation."[44]

Although experimental reason seems incapable of inferring much of the religious hypothesis by reasoning directly from the observed state of the universe, it may be capable of providing rational support for theology by certifying indirect evidence for the hypothesis. Such would be the case if experimental reason could certify the veracity of human testimony for the historicity of miracles, which in turn guarantee the divine origin of revelatory religion. This confirmatory role of allegedly historical events was in Hume's day, and often still is, the interpretation put on miracles by theologians and religious philosophers.[45]

Whether miracles can play such an indirect role in the verification of the religious hypothesis is what Hume sets out to examine in his famous essay on miracles (*Enquiry* X). This part of the *Enquiry* seems to have attracted wider attention than most other parts; but its role in the mapping of his mental geography seems also to have been widely overlooked. Usually the essay is taken as an attempt on Hume's part to "attract attention, and excite that 'murmur among the zealots' by which the author desired to be distinguished"; and, as an exercise in polemics, the essay is dismissed as irrelevant to the epistemological theme of the *Enquiry*.[46] Hume himself, however, clearly states the epistemological purpose of the

44. *Ibid.*, 146.
45. See E. A. Burtt, *Types of Religious Philosophy* (New York: Harper, 1939), pp. 122 ff., 136, 150, 158 f., 165; J. M. Creed and J. S. B. Smith, *Religious Thought in the Eighteenth Century* (Cambridge: Cambridge University Press, 1934), pp. 53 ff., 86ff.
46. See Selby-Bigge's introduction to the *Enquiry*, pp. viii and xii; N. K. Smith in D. Hume, *Dialogues concerning Natural Religion* (Edinburgh: Nelson, 1947), pp. 46 and 49 f.; and A. E. Taylor, chapter 9.

essay as being concerned with the question of whether "human testimony can have such force as to prove a miracle, and make it a just foundation for any such system of religion".[47]

His negative answer to this question is based on, and is strictly consistent with, the epistemological principles enunciated in his doctrine regarding experimental reason. The conclusions attained by the use of this faculty, Hume has already argued, are only probable; and the probability may be expressed as a numerical function of the quantitative nature of the relevant experience. Frequent and unexceptioned experience provides a degree of probability approaching 1, but still less than the certainty attainable by deductive inference or that afforded by arguments from complete enumeration. Hume designates the highest degree of empirical probability "proofs" in distinction to the lesser "probabilities" afforded by inductive inferences drawn from fewer or from more variable experiences. Thus, to cite Hume's examples, we have proof of the incendiary properties of fire but only a probability for the purgative properties of rhubarb. Those natural operations for whose regularity experience affords empirical proof are termed "laws of nature."[48]

The degree of probability attaching to the veracity of human testimony does not usually attain quite the standard of a proof; but considering the good repute and tested honesty of individual witnesses, certain testimony may attain even that high degree of credibility. This, however, will be the case only when there is nothing in the testimony itself or in the circumstances under which the testimony is delivered that would vitiate its credi-

47. *Enquiry*, p. 127.
48. *Ibid.*, pp. 56 n., 57, 127.

bility.[49] If, on the other hand, the attested fact is incompatible with, or foreign to, previous experience, its credibility will be reduced inasmuch as it relies for its credence on experimental reason. The evidence for the unlikelihood of the attested event will be contrary evidence to that for the reliability of human testimony; and the net probability of the latter will be a residue obtained by subtracting the probability of the former.

Hume discusses two genera of unlikely events, natural and supernatural. The former are characterized by their rarity or unprecedentedness; the latter, by being contrary to experience or violations of the laws of nature—terms that are interchangeable for Hume since laws of nature are what "firm and unalterable experience has established". Among the supernatural events, Hume distinguishes two species: the magical and the miraculous.[50] Both species are of a kind, and differ only in the circumstances under which they occur: the miraculous in connection with claims of mediate or immediate divine intervention, and the magical unconnected with such claims. Hume thus defines a miracle as *"a transgression of a law of nature by a particular volition of the Deity, or by the interposition of some invisible agent."*[51] What Hume aims to question in *Enquiry X* is whether this species of event can be supported by sufficient empirical evidence to constitute indirect experimental evidence for

---

49. *Ibid.*, pp. 112 f., 114, and X *passim*.
50. Hume's practice of calling both the genus and the two species "miraculous" has resulted in criticism that would be obviated by more consistent terminology. In fact, Hume's first definition (p. 114) relates to the supernatural, and his second (p. 115) to the miraculous. His examples also refer variously to the genus and its species. Taylor, who complains that Hume manufactures new definitions to suit his purpose (p. 337) could be answered by reference to the different types of event that Hume considers with each new definition.
51. *Enquiry*, p. 115.

the truth of the religious hypothesis which miracles are claimed to attest.

That it cannot be so supported follows, in Hume's view, from the fact that the evidence for the occurrence of the miracle, that is, the evidence of human testimony, is incompatible with the evidence to the contrary, that is, the evidence for the inviolability of natural law. Granting even that evidence in favor of the former amounts to a proof, that for the latter is of an equal magnitude. Consequently, the residual probability in favor of the reliability of miraculous occurrences can under optimum conditions amount to 0. This is to say that the determinations of experimental reason on this question are inconclusive:

> Our evidence, then, for the truth of the Christian religion is less than the evidence for the truth of our senses . . . when they are considered merely as external evidences.
> A miracle can never be proved, so as to be the foundation of a system of religion.
> No testimony is sufficient to establish a miracle, unless the testimony be of such a kind, that its falsehood would be more miraculous, than the fact, which it endeavours to establish; and even in that case there is a mutual destruction of arguments, and the superior only gives us an assurance suitable to that degree of force, which remains, after deducting the inferior.[52]

In his secondary arguments Hume goes on to contend that the degree of probability for the veracity of human testimony concerning the miraculous has, as a matter of historical fact, been considerably less than that for the regularity of nature. Thus, an experimental calculus tends to falsify rather than to verify historical accounts of miracles. But this extension is not essential to his case.

---

52. *Ibid.*, pp. 109, 127, 115 f.

It suffices for the purpose of his investigation into the applicability of experimental reason to theology to show that the residual probability in favor of the religious hypothesis is at best far short of empirical proof. Of course, appeal to God as the omnipotent agent of miracles is not a legitimate device, for this assumes the question at issue—whether the proof for miracles can provide proof for the religious hypothesis. It is this, Hume maintains, that experimental reason is incapable of doing:

> I am the better pleased with the method of reasoning here delivered, as I think it may serve to confound those dangerous friends or disguised enemies to the *Christian Religion,* who have undertaken to defend it by the principles of human reason . . . and it is a sure method of exposing it to put it to such a trial as it is, by no means, fitted to endure.[53]

---

53. *Ibid.,* pp. 129 f.

6
Perception

Perception and Percepts

To hold that abstract reason and experimental reason exhaust the limits of rational knowledge is not to say that they exhaust the limits of the human understanding. Hume's reiterated references to the incapacity of *reason* to elicit conclusions in the fields of aesthetics and ethics, divinity and perception assert no more than that such conclusions are neither demonstrably nor probably calculable; but this does not entail that they are therefore past human understanding. On the contrary, since Hume holds that there are objects of the understanding other than relations of ideas and matters of fact, and since the varieties of reason are limited only to relations of ideas and to matters of fact, it follows that for Hume there exist other, noninferential, modes of understanding. Of these, perhaps the most important is what Hume calls

99

perception; and the objects of this faculty are the perceptions, or percepts.

The only clue to the meaning of this generic term is provided by Hume's definitions of its species and the examples he gives of its sub-species or classes. Kemp Smith uses the term "components of experience"[1] as an expression roughly synonymous with Hume's "perceptions." Under this head are included all those mental phenomena and stimuli with which we are supposed to be immediately, that is, noninferentially, acquainted. This genus is perhaps best understood if we consider it as the sum of what Hume claims to be its component species.

One such species consists of the impressions, which Hume defines as "all our more lively perceptions, when we hear, or see, or feel, or love, or hate, or desire, or will."[2] The impressions fall into two classes. The first is coextensive with what is called (by philosophers who maintain the representative theory of perception) sense data or immediate objects of awareness. In Hume's scheme, these form the class of sensations or, as he sometimes calls them, objects of external sense. Between the dualist's sense data and Hume's sensations there is this major distinction that, while the former are taken as evidence of mediate objects of awareness, the latter are not associated by Hume with any such entities that act as their source. More precisely, Hume maintains that if there are such entities, say, material bodies, then their existence can neither be inferred by reason nor apprehended by sense perception:

1. Kemp Smith, *The Philosophy of David Hume* (London: Macmillan, 1964), chapter 5.
2. D. Hume, *Enquiries concerning the Human Understanding and the Principles of Morals*, ed. L. A. Selby-Bigge, 2nd ed. (Oxford: Oxford University Press, 1902), p. 18.

When men follow this blind and powerful instinct of nature, they always suppose the very images, presented by the senses, to be the external objects. . . . But this universal and primary opinion of all men is soon destroyed by the slightest philosophy, which teaches us, that nothing can ever be present to the mind but an image or perception.[3]

The second class of impression comprises what Hume calls the sentiments (or objects of internal sense). These might be described as the psychological counterparts of the sensory sensations. They include such feelings, assuming that they can be identified, as are associated with the "psychological commotions" not directly evoked by the stimulation of sense receptors. They may, however, be indirectly associated with such stimulation. The sentiment of jealousy, for example, can be aroused by a visual or an auditory sensation.

The second species of percept includes ideas, which Hume defines as "the less lively perceptions, of which we are conscious, when we reflect on any of those sensations or movements above mentioned."[4] This species comprises two classes: ideas of the memory and ideas of the imagination, terms which Hume apparently considers familiar enough not to require independent definition. His treatment of the species of ideas consists in a discussion of the features that distinguish it from, and relate it to, the species of impressions. It is a peculiarly difficult and contentious part of Hume's theory. Since it is central to Hume's thesis that percepts are the basic elements in our experience of the universe, he deliberately omits any reference to what would normally be taken as the criterion for distinguishing between impressions and ideas: namely,

3. *Ibid.*, pp. 151 f.
4. *Ibid.*, p. 18.

the objective or publicly accessible nature of impressions or of their source.

What he offers instead is, first, a quantitative distinction which permits impressions to be recognized by the greater degree of "vivacity," "force," or "liveliness" with which they are perceived as compared to that with which ideas are perceived. One difficulty that this criterion encounters is the problem of mensuration. It is not clear at what precise degree of vivacity—or even how we are to establish at what degree of vivacity—a percept is transformed from membership in the species of ideas into membership in the species of impressions. In itself, this is not an insuperable difficulty, for it need not follow from the fact that a proposed distinction is not precisely determinable that the distinction is non-existent. But Hume admits a further weakness in the doctrine when he concedes that an idea may have the vivacity of an impression to a mind "disordered by disease or madness."[5] Apart from blurring the quantitative nature of the distinction, this concession seems to be inconsistent with it.

A second distinction between the species of percepts involves the claim that the ideas are "weaker copies" or "images" of impressions. Experimental proof of this is provided (a) by the fact that all simple ideas (that is, ideas that are not analyzable into component ideas) can be traced to antecedent impressions; and (b) by the fact that a sensory deficiency, either organic or circumstantial, results in the irremedial absence of the correlative idea.[6] This empirically necessary association of every idea with an impression is extended by Hume into a theory of meaning. It is, roughly, a label theory of meaning which

5. *Ibid.*, p. 17.
6. *Ibid.*, pp. 18 ff., 62, 78.

demands that for every term there shall be a determinate idea, one which can be traced back to an impression.[7] All definition must, thus, be ultimately ostensive, but with the terms attaching not to things but rather to impressions.

Against (*a*) it may be argued that the task of relating each individual term to a determinate idea derived from an impression presents insuperable procedural difficulties. In a reference to this problem, Quine[8] suggests that the difficulty might be overcome by accepting as basic linguistic units not only words but also extended sentences whose meaning is learnt "by a direct conditioning of the whole utterance to some sensory stimulation." In such cases, then, the meaning of an individual word for which no appropriate impression can be isolated may be considered as representing a fragment of the sentence learned as a whole.

A more fundamental objection is that of Flew[9] who argues that the whole enterprise of trying to trace the meaning of terms back to impressions is, if not erroneous, at least superfluous. He points out that a person with an organic defect, say, blindness, which prevents him from experiencing a specific type of impression, say, color, can still form ideas of what he has not experienced through the intermediacy of instruments. Such a person may utilize a color-meter which clicks in characteristic ways in the presence of different colors. So far as the use of color terminology goes, the blind man will be on an equal footing with the sighted man notwithstanding that the

7. *Ibid.*, pp. 22, 62, 74, 158 n.
8. W. V. O. Quine, *Word and Object* (Cambridge, Mass.: M.I.T. Press, 1960), p. 9.
9. A. Flew, *Hume's Philosophy of Belief* (London: Routledge and Kegan Paul, 1961), pp. 40 ff.

former has had no experience of the relevant impression. Both will be equally well informed in which cases it is correct to say "*x* is red" and in which cases it is incorrect.

Flew uses this as an argument against (*b*), which Hume takes to prove the necessity for sensible experience as the criterion for the determinacy of ideas and as the bearer of meaning. Flew's objection, however, does not seem to me to refute the dependence of meaning on impressions. First, even if the blind man can depend on the machine to inform him of variations in color, it still does not release him (as Flew suggests it does) from dependence on impressions: it merely shifts the dependence from one variety of impression, the visual, to another, the auditory. Second, it seems at least arguable whether it is correct to say that the sighted and the blind man mean the same when they both utter "*x* is red." For the blind man, the locution has at least the additional meaning that his apprehension of redness is mediated by the machine. Third, even if it is conceded that knowledge of when and when not to apply a locution is sufficient ground for adjudging its meaning to be known, then the blind man may be said to know the meaning of such relatively primitive color locutions as "*x* is red"; but it is doubtful whether by the same criterion he can be said to comprehend such locutions as "I find pale blue rather restful on the eyes."

There remains another kind of difficulty with regard to the theory of perception. This concerns the sense in which ideas are supposed to be images of impressions. One way of interpreting the relationship is to consider the idea as some sort of pictorial or iconic representation of the impression, as a photograph is a representation of the person pictured—except that the idea is a mental rather than a material representation of its correlative impression. One variety or another of the iconic interpretation has dominated exegesis of Hume; and it is against an iconic theory of perception attributed to Hume that much of the criticism of his theory of perception is directed. Flew,[10] for example, holds that Hume's theory cannot correctly describe the relation of ideas to impressions in all cases because, while it is true that some people ideate in pictorial images, many others think in abstract or nonpictorial terms.

This, and allied criticism,[11] would be quite valid if Hume actually held that the relationship was an iconic one. The notion that this was Hume's intention arises, I believe, from a literal reading of Hume's metaphorical description of ideas as "mental images" of impressions, and from an undue emphasis by commentators on examples drawn from visual perceptions which easily lend themselves to an iconic interpretation. But of course Hume's list of percepts includes much more than visual experiences, and it becomes nonsensical to speak of iconic representations of, say, olfactory or gustatory impressions, and even more so of emotional or volitional ones. The characterization of ideas as weaker copies or fainter images of impressions makes more sense, and is more consistent with Hume's whole treatment of the relationship in *Enquiry III,* if the noun *image* is taken in a figurative sense and emphasis is shifted from the noun to the adjec-

10. *Ibid.,* p. 35 f., and see chapter 2.
11. See, for example, D. G. C. MacNabb, *David Hume: His Theory of Knowledge and Morality* (London: Hutchinson's University Library, 1951), pp. 35 f.; F. Zabeeh, *Hume: Precursor of Modern Empiricism* (The Hague: Martinus Nijhoff, 1960), pp. 69 ff.; A. H. Basson, *David Hume* (Harmondsworth: Penguin Books, 1958), pp. 30 ff.; E. J. Furlong, "Imagination in Hume's *Treatise* and *Enquiry concerning Human Understanding,*" *Philosophy* 36 (1961): 62; and H. A. Prichard, *Knowledge and Perception* (Oxford: Oxford University Press, 1950), p. 174.

tive *fainter*. The sense that this will then convey is that
the idea of a visual impression is a weaker and more
fleeting picture of the thing imagined than is the experience of the thing seen; to remember a taste is to
have a weaker perception of that taste (but not so in-
discernible that thinking of it cannot make the mouth
water) ; and to think of a past grudge is not to feel the
original fury, but still to experience faint stirrings of
anger. If such an interpretation fails to remove all the
difficulties inherent in Hume's theory of perception, it
does at least remove those that cluster round an iconic
interpretation of the theory.

Hume claims that ideas are marked by yet a third
differentia, one whose discovery he considered to be his
main contribution to epistemology. The primary percepts,
impressions, impinge on the consciousness in disordered
succession—a kaleidoscopic jumble of sensations and sentiments that provide awareness only of the momentary
experience.[12] But it is obviously untrue to say that our
only perception of the world consists in this "chaos of
fragmentary things" (Helen Keller) or to suggest that
the patterns which do emerge from the shards of experience are the product of deliberate reason. Percepts are
integrated into wholes; but Hume maintains that the
integration occurs not at the level of sensible experience but rather at the level of ideas. We are saved from
kaleidoscopism by the associative powers of the memory
and the imagination:

> It is evident that there is a principle of connexion between the
> different thoughts or ideas of the mind, and that, in their ap-

---

12. D. Hume, *An Abstract of A Treatise of Human Nature*, ed. Keynes
and Sraffa (Cambridge: Cambridge University Press, 1938) , p. 31 and
Enquiry, pp. 42, 55, 63, 73.

pearance to the memory or imagination, they introduce each other with a certain degree of method and regularity . . . Even in our wildest and most wandering reveries, nay in our very dreams, we shall find, if we reflect, that the imagination ran not altogether at adventures, but that there was still a connexion upheld among the different ideas, which succeeded each other.[13]

Hume's quarrel with the sort of realism exemplified by G. E. Moore[14] concerns the question of the separability of the elements of perceptual experience. Both would agree that we always perceive ordered wholes. Hume takes this as evidence for the transformation of distinct impressions into ideas and the integration of these ideas into wholes by the action upon the ideas of the associative powers of the understanding. Moore takes it as evidence for the claim that what we perceive *is* wholes, a fact reflected in the language of perception: "I see my hand"; and not, "I experience an amorphous pinkness . . . and this experience I call 'seeing my hand.' "

The associative elements which, when added to other ideas and impressions, provide our percepts with their coherence are resemblance, contiguity, and cause.[15] Hume's theory requires that these elements be themselves traced back to impressions since, failing this, the very terms would be "absolutely without meaning," and since these elements are themselves perceptual particulars which combine with other perceptual particulars. Hume's solution to this problem is to find the original impression for the idea of cause in a sentiment evoked by the regular

13. *Enquiry*, p. 23.
14. G. E. Moore, "The Refutation of Idealism", *Mind*, 12 (1903).
15. *Ibid.*, pp. 23 f. and 50 ff. Norman Kemp Smith (*The Philosophy of David Hume*, p. 250n.) reduces Hume's associative principles to one, namely "the law of reintegration": "Any part of a single state of mind tends, if reproduced, to re-instate the remainder; or Any element tends to reproduce those elements with which it has formed one state of mind."

conjunction of similar successive pairs of events. It seems
to have escaped the notice of Hume's critics that no solution is offered for the equally mysterious origins of the
remaining associative ideas. But assuming that resemblance and contiguity, as well as cause, are cashable as
sentiments, his theory of perception results in the conclusion that the apparent order of our percepts is one
imposed by the perceiving agent: " 'Twill be easy to
conceive of what vast consequence these principles must
be in the science of human nature, if we consider, that
so far as regards the mind, [the associative ideas] are
the only links that bind the parts of the universe together.
. . . They are really to us the cement of the universe."[16]

Perception and the Objects of Rational Knowledge

Of the five modes of understanding, perception is, for
Hume, the most fundamental. All the others involve a
marshalling of impressions and ideas in various configura-
tions, but however remote the final product of such a
configuration may seem to be from its original perceptual
material, it is ultimately analyzable into component percepts derived in the first instance from impressions. Differences among modes of understanding depend on variations in the mix and in the transformation or processing
of this original perceptual material. Thus the validity of
a conclusion pertaining to any given mode of understanding is established both by examining the correctness of
the procedures involved in reaching the conclusion and
by resolving argument and conclusion into their perceptual elements. The crucial stage of this resolution is
the analysis of the components into impressions. Unless

16. *Abstract*, p. 31.

this final step is possible the entire argument under consideration is rendered literally senseless. Even in abstract reason, which deals exclusively with relations among ideas, impressions are the controlling factor: they are used, not to determine the correctness of the reasoning process involved, but to establish the credentials of the ideas operated upon in that process. The doctrine of the derivation of ideas from impressions accounts for Hume's peculiar treatment of paradoxes emanating from apparent contradictions between sense experience and mathematical abstractions (See chapter 4 above).

The bearing of perceptual experience, particularly of impressions, on experimental reason is more intimate. First, the analyzability of chains of reasoning into component perceptions and, ultimately, impressions obtains not only for abstract, but also for experimental, arguments. In the case of the latter, Hume claims to have made such an analysis possible by tracing to its parent impression the idea common to all such arguments (this assumes, of course, that the other elements appearing as variables in experimental arguments present no reductive problem) :

> When many uniform instances appear, and the same object is always followed by the same event; we then begin to entertain the notion of cause and connexion. We then *feel* a new sentiment or impression, to wit, a customary connexion in the thought or imagination between one object and its usual attendant; and this sentiment is the original of that idea which we seek for.[17]

Second, while abstract reason deals exclusively with ideas, experimental reason normally operates on perceptual elements at least one of which is a present impression (or

---

17. *Enquiry*, p. 78. For Hume's arguments against the possibility of other impressions as being the source of our idea of cause, see *ibid.*, VII,

the present memory of a past impression) with which the reasoning agent is directly acquainted:

> All our reasonings concerning fact are of the same nature. . . . It is constantly supposed that there is a connexion between the present fact and that which is inferred from it.[18]

Third, the whole experimental calculus of probability is a mathematical description of the degree of vividness with which the component ideas are provided by the relative frequency of their parent impressions:

> When the mind looks forward to discover the event, which may result from the throw of . . . a dye, it considers the turning up of each particular side as alike probable. . . . But finding a greater number of sides concur in the one event than in the other, the mind is carried more frequently to that event. . . . This concurrence of several views in one particular event begets immediately, by an inexplicable contrivance of nature, the sentiment of belief, and gives that event the advantage over its antagonist, which is supported by a smaller number of views, and recurs less frequently to the mind. . . . The case is the same with the probability of causes, as with that of chances.[19]

Thus, in contrast to the subsidiary role played by impressions in the field of abstract reason, they are integral to experimental reason, both as elements entering into, or forming part of, its calculations and as factors determining the validity of these calculations.

Perception and Theology

There remains to be discussed the relationship of perception to value judgments and to the religious hypothesis. Consideration of the former is reserved for chapter 7

18. *Ibid.*, pp. 26 f.; see also pp. 45 f.
19. *Ibid.*, p. 57.

below. As for the latter, it would be reasonable to expect that Hume's theory of perception should favor, or at least be compatible with, a theology based on the argument from religious experience. The proponents of such a theology claim to have knowledge of God on the impeccably Humean grounds of a direct experience of the deity through some impression that affords evidence to the sense or sentiment of the divine existence.

Whether Hume would have to acknowledge the infrangibility of the argument from religious experience actually involves two distinct though related questions: whether a secondhand claim to such an experience is weighty enough to warrant credence; and whether a firsthand experience of this nature is convincing proof of the religious hypothesis to the person undergoing the experience. Philosophical discussion of the problem is generally confined to the former, that is, the weaker, version of the argument;[20] and it is not difficult to show— as Hume has shown in his essay on miracles—that the balance of credibility does not weigh in favor of the reputed religious experience. The report that a religious experience has occurred is not itself a religious experience; hence it cannot count as an impression validating the religious hypothesis by perceptual evidence:

> Our evidence, then, for the truth of the *Christian* religion is less than the evidence for the truth of our senses; because, even in the first authors of our religion, it was no greater; and it is evident it must diminish in passing from them to their disciples; nor can any one rest such confidence in their testimony, as in the immediate object of his senses.[21]

---

20. See, for example, M. Scriven, *Primary Philosophy* (New York: McGraw-Hill, 1966), pp. 136 f.; and Flew, *God and Philosophy* (London: Hutchinson, 1966), pp. 124 ff.

21. *Enquiry*, p. 109.

Hume's theory of perception seems to permit a counter-argument to disbelief in reports of a religious experience along the lines that such incredulity is analogous to that with which a blind man might regard reports of a visual experience. That is, one might err in disbelieving a claim for the occurrence of an impression merely because one happens to be congenitally incapable of experiencing such an impression. In point of fact, however, the blind man —unlike the religious sceptic—does not disbelieve reports of an experience which he is incapable of sharing. The difference between the two cases lies in this, that the blind man, unlike the religious sceptic, lives among people the majority of whom concur in relating mutually compatible accounts of direct visual experiences. Experience has taught him to trust these accounts, both because there is no apparent reason for those who relate them to deceive him and, more important, because the truth of the accounts is circumstantially supported by the success of predictions based on such accounts.

Such a justification for credence forms part of Hume's argument in *Enquiry* X. It seems to lead to the consequence that belief in the religious hypothesis would be justified on the argument from religious experience if a majority of mankind concurred in avowing such experience, if they had no interest in lying about it, and if the hypothesis were circumstantially evidenced by predictive success. One may carry the analogy between religious and visual experience even a stage further by asking whether it would not serve to convince the sceptic if, like a blind man restored to sight, he were granted the faculty of sensing such an experience himself. This is to broach the second of our two questions: namely, whether a firsthand religious experience, than which there can be no stronger evidence, is sufficient to prove the religious hypothesis.

The answer, from the point of view of Hume's theory of perception, is that even a firsthand experience is insufficient to establish the hypothesis. The religious experience, if we are to credit those who have reported on it from first hand, consists of an awareness of an emanative or an immanent entity whose presence is manifest at a specific level, or to a specific faculty, of the subject's consciousness.[22] Granting that the experience is neither illusory nor hallucinatory, and granting also that its authenticity need not be established by its being reproducible or amenable to public inspection, the experience itself can convey no more than that there is such an entity present to the consciousness. What the perception cannot establish is that the entity is omnipotent or providential or infinitely good or the creator of the universe, or that it punishes the wicked and rewards the just in an afterlife. These accretions to the original perception of the divine presence are inferences regarding its nature; and, as such, they are subject to Hume's criticism of experimental arguments for the religious hypothesis.

---

22. See E. Underhill, *Mysticism* (London: Methuen, 1960), pt. 1, chapter 5.

7

Taste

Taste and Value Judgments

There is little discussion in the first *Enquiry* of that faculty by which we distinguish "vice and virtue" and "beauty and deformity."[1] Although *Enquiry VIII* is ostensibly about a topic closely related to ethics, it is in fact largely concerned with a discussion of causality and with the demolition of yet another spurious source for the notion of causality—the feeling supposedly engendered by the exercise of free will. The direct references that Hume does make to the faculty employed in evaluative judgments amount to a germinal account of the moral sense or, more correctly, the moral sentiment theory elaborated in the second *Enquiry*.

Reference has already been made to the inapplicability

---

1. D. Hume, *Enquiries concerning the Human Understanding and concerning the Principles of Morals*, ed. L. A. Selby-Bigge, 2nd ed. (Oxford: Oxford University Press, 1902), pp. 102 f.

of abstract reason to value judgments, and to the incidental and auxiliary role played in this field by experimental reason.[2] Hume contends that value judgments in
both ethics and aesthetics are the expression of an immediate impression relative to a unique sentiment:

> . . . A late Philosopher has taught us, by the most convincing
> Arguments, that Morality is nothing in the abstract Nature
> of Things, but is entirely relative to the Sentiment or mental
> Taste of each particular Being; in the same Manner as the
> Distinctions of sweet and bitter, hot and cold, arise from the
> particular Feeling of each Sense or Organ.[3]

Strictly speaking, therefore, mental taste belongs among
the percepts; and it is as a specialized percept that Hume
clearly intends it to be viewed:

> Moral Perceptions . . . ought not to be class'd with the
> [rational] Operations of the Understanding, but with the
> Tastes or Sentiments;[4]

and

> [It is] the various species of sentiment which discriminate
> vice and virtue.[5]

Nevertheless we are justified in considering it apart from
the other percepts by the fact that Hume singles out this
percept from the others in the envoy of the *Enquiry* (pp.
163-65) and by the fact that Hume attributes certain

---

2. It is incidental because the determinations of mental taste coincide
contingently with what experimental reason calculates to be socially
beneficial or harmful; and it is auxiliary because experimental reason
can inform us only of the means of attaining our ethical ends, but has
no part in selecting these ends. (See chapter 5 above, and second *Enquiry, I*.)
3. *Enquiry* (ed. Mossner), p. 18 n.
4. *Ibid.*, p. 18 n.
5. *Enquiry*, p. 10.

unique characteristics to this faculty in both the first and the second *Enquiries.*

The status of mental taste as a percept implies that the determinations of the ethical faculty are subjective, or relative to the perceiver, in the sense that moral judgments do not refer to some property that inheres in the object of perceptual contemplation, but rather that they reflect the sentiments evoked in the moral agent by contemplation of the object. Both Broad[6] and Lillie[7] argue that Hume is saved from ethical subjectivism by his supplementary thesis which relates the terms good and bad not only to the immediate sentiment of the perceiver but also to what is deemed good and bad by the majority of mankind. Broad goes on to deduce from this principle the consequence that the settlement of ethical disputes reduces to a statistical technique: "x is good" is true if most men would feel the sentiment of approval on contemplating x, and it is false if most men would not feel this sentiment. Broad implies that he might accept a thoroughgoing subjective theory whose consequence is the irreconcilability of ethical disputes, but not one that entails the repugnant consequence which he attributes to Hume's theory.

The evidence, however, does not support the view that Hume's theory is rendered objective by the principle of "the common consent of mankind." It is a principle of which Hume makes a special use, and this not only with regard to mental taste but with regard to all perception. Hume's solution to the private language problem, which seems inseparable from any sense data theory, is not to

_____

6. C. D. Broad, *Five Types of Ethical Theory* (London: Routledge and Kegan Paul, 1930), pp. 84 ff.
7. W. Lillie, *An Introduction to Ethics* (London: Methuen, 1955), pp. 110 f.

reject the privacy of sense data—he is committed to the
view that these are "entirely relative to the Sentiment . . .
of each particular Being"—but to make locutions regarding private sense data mutually intelligible by postulating
a perceptual apparatus that is more or less common to
all members of the human species:

> The faculties of the mind are supposed to be naturally alike
> in every individual; otherwise nothing could be more fruit-
> less than to reason or dispute together; it were impossible, if
> men affix the same ideas to their terms, that they could so
> long form different opinions of the same subject; especially
> when they communicate their views.[8]

This postulate is not to be confused with epistemic
publicity: in fact, it is an alternative to epistemic publicity. Again, like the supposed coincidence between the
determinations of mental taste and the experimental calculus of social utility, that between the mental taste of a
particular being and the majority of mankind is contingent. The ultimate criterion is therefore not objective.
It need coincide neither with considerations of utility
nor with the majority view: it is still the private sentiment
of approval or opprobrium that arbitrates in the evaluative sphere. Hume is quite unequivocal in his assessment
that where there occurs a contrariety between the judgments of taste and of reason, between the subjective and
the objective, between the private sentiment and the
common consent of mankind, it is the former that prevails:

> What though philosophical meditations establish a different
> opinion or conjecture; that everything is right with regard
> to the WHOLE, and that the qualities, which disturb society,
> are, in the main, as beneficial, and are as suitable to the pri-

---

8. *Enquiry*, p. 80.

mary intention of nature as those which more directly pro-
mote its happiness and welfare? Are such remote and uncertain speculations able to counterbalance the sentiments
which arise from the natural and immediate view of the
objects? . . . . Both [ethical and aesthetic] distinctions are
founded in the natural sentiments of the human mind.[9]

Whether such a personalized ethic or its associated personalized theory of perception is philosophically tenable
is another question; but at least it does not commit the
crude naturalistic error of submitting ethical disputes to
a popularity poll for decision.

Taste and Theology

Since taste is an impression, the relation of that faculty
to spheres other than value judgments is implicitly contained in Hume's discussion of the relationship of perception in general to these other spheres. The *Enquiry*
does, however, refer explicitly to the inapplicability of
ethical judgments to the validation of elements of the
religious hypothesis.

Although it is not so common as the effort to derive
ethics from theology, the reverse procedure—the derivation of theology from ethics—has also been attempted by
various philosophers. Kant, for example, considers it an
inseparable consequence of the quest for moral perfection
by imperfect beings that there shall exist the possibility
of attaining this perfection, if not in the finitude of
earthly space and mortal span, then in an immaterial
environment and an infinite existence. In Kant's theory
"pure practical reason" requires that the coincidence of
virtue and happiness be a necessary one. But since, in

---

9. *Ibid.*, pp. 102 f.; see also p. 165.

the phenomenal sphere, it is patently a contingent coincidence, it follows for Kant that we need to postulate a perfectly just agent who will harmonize virtue and happiness in the noumenal sphere. Thus, from the facts of phenomenal ethics Kant claims to be able to derive the immortality of the soul and the existence of God.[10]

While Hume's formulation is rather different from that of Kant, he too considers the same two questions explored by his successor: whether extra-ethical conclusions can be deduced from ethical premises; and whether a particular providence and a future state can be inferred from the requirement that justice be fulfilled. Kant's answer is in the affirmative on both scores, but he concedes that his conclusion is "a *theoretical* proposition, not demonstrable as such."[11] For Hume, since it is neither demonstrable nor deductively inferable, the conclusion does not follow at all:

Are there any marks of a distributive justice in the world? If you answer in the affirmative, I conclude, that, since justice here exerts itself, it is satisfied. If you reply in the negative, I conclude, that you have then no reason to ascribe justice, in our sense of it, to the gods. If you hold a medium between affirmation and negation, by saying, that the justice of the gods, at present, exerts itself in part, but not in its full extent; I answer, that you have no reason to give it any particular extent, but only so far as you see it, *at present*, exert itself.[12]

In effect, this is an anticipatory reply to Kant. Hume would hold that if virtue and happiness are found to coincide only contingently, then the contingent nature of the coincidence will simply have to be accepted. The

10. I. Kant, *Critique of Practical Reason and Other Works on the Theory of Ethics.* Trans. T. K. Abbott, 2nd ed. (London: Longmans, 1909), pp. 218–28.
11. *Ibid.*, p. 219.
12. *Enquiry*, pp. 141 f.

coincidence is not made necessary simply by virtue of the fact that we *want* it to be necessary or that we deem it to be necessary so as to redress the balance of justice. Thus, it does not follow, and we cannot make it follow, from ethical premises that there is a supreme arbiter who assures the equitable distribution of just deserts that happen not to be meted out in this life, nor does it follow that there is a future state where these deserts are meted out. For such conclusions to be justly inferred, it would need to be shown that the relationship between actions having an ethical content and the just retribution for such actions is an analytic relationship, or that this relationship is known from experience to be uniform. Kant does not claim, and Hume denies, that the relationship is either logically necessary or experimentally probable.

Even if it were the case that one relationship or the other obtained, this would still be insufficient to validate the inference from ethical premises to theological conclusion. For the fact that virtue must logically be rewarded, or the fact that virtue is always rewarded, does not logically entail the proposition that this operation is effected by God, nor does it entail the proposition that an eternal span is required for its attainment. Nor is it true that either of these theological propositions is rendered highly probable in the calculus of experimental reason by the observed frequency of conjunctions among ethical actions and their due reward.

Finally, even if a logical or an experimental bond could be established between compensatory redress on the one hand and the existence of God and the immortality of the soul on the other, such an inference would still not suffice to establish God's oneness, his creative power, his universal benevolence, his omnipotence, his omniscience, or any element of the religious hypothesis other than that a deity (or deities) provide compensatory redress in eternity for actions having an ethical content.

8
Faith

Hume's Religious Scepticism

It is widely held that Hume's writings on religion and
the implications of his epistemological doctrines constitute, at least implicitly, a rejection or denial of the
religious hypothesis:

> The teaching of the *Dialogues* is much more sheerly negative
> than has generally been held. . . . He is consciously, and de-
> liberately, attacking the "religious hypothesis," and through
> it religion as such. . . . Their influence . . . has been of the
> same wide-ranging character as, by universal consent, has
> been exercised by Hume's no less negatively inspired *Treatise
> of Human Nature* and by his *Enquiries*.[1]

This seems to be a fair inference from Hume's pronounce-
ments on the insufficiency of any of the faculties so far

---

1. N. K. Smith, in the preface to D. Hume, *Dialogues concerning
Natural Religion* (Edinburgh: Nelson, 1947).

considered to establish the religious hypothesis. It may even be the case, as MacNabb takes it to be, that "the main enemy in the *Enquiry* is not metaphysics but religion."[2]

While the plausibility of such an inference is not in question, it is at least worth considering an alternative interpretation, one which Hume ostensibly advocates. Hume's doctrines concerning the relation between the four faculties and the religious hypothesis lead to the conclusion that, while none of the faculties is capable of establishing the hypothesis, none of them flatly contradicts the hypothesis: the faculties are simply inapplicable to the hypothesis. Hume's strictures in the *Enquiry* are reserved not for the religious hypothesis but for attempts to prove the hypothesis by means of rational or perceptual or moral arguments. In the envoy, it is not books of theology that Hume advocates committing to the flames, but theological works that contain abstract reasoning on topics other than quantity or number, or experimental reasoning on topics other than matters of fact and existence. Even the "purple peroration" with which he concludes *Enquiry X* says in substance—even if it makes the point in flamboyant terms—only that, judged by the canons of experimental reason, there is a residual probability against credence in reports of miracles, the occurrence of transubstantiation, and like Christian articles of faith: "Mere reason is insufficient to convince us of [the] veracity [of the Christian religion]," and its miracles are "contrary to custom and experience."[3]

It might be argued that, ostensibly at least, the denial

2. "David Hume", *The Encyclopedia of Philosophy* 4:75.
3. D. Hume, *Enquiries concerning the Human Understanding and concerning the Principles of Morals*, ed. L. A. Selby-Bigge, 2nd ed. (Oxford: Oxford University Press, 1902), p. 131.

of the religious hypothesis is incompatible with Hume's stated doctrines. Abstractly considered, all existential propositions are equally true; therefore the proposition "God exists" may be true. The conclusions of experimental reason are all more or less probable; hence theological propositions, insofar as they are existential, are at least possibly true. What we know from perception is fortuitously limited to what we happen to have apprehended by sense or sentiment; and there remains the possibility that we may experience new percepts related to religion. The inference from ethics to theology is a case of unjust reasoning; but unjust reasoning does not necessarily render the conclusion false, any more than just reasoning (as in the case of the Indian prince[4]) renders it true. The conclusion that appears to be most consonant with these doctrines is the view that, as far as it lies in the power of these faculties to determine, there is no positive evidence for the religious hypothesis, and that it is therefore proper to withhold credence from the hypothesis.

Faith and Theology

This consequence does not exclude the possibility of our apprehending religious cognitions by other means. If we accept Hume's doctrines at face value, we find that he does provide a cognitive medium through which we are able to acquiesce in religious beliefs. This medium is the faculty of faith.[5] What distinguishes his treatment of this from his treatment of the other irrational faculties is that with regard to faith he makes no effort to account

4. *Ibid.*, pp. 113 f.
5. *Ibid.*, pp. 130, 131, 135, 165.

for, or even claim, mutual intelligibility or a common human body of religious cognitions. In the case of perception, he postulated a perceptual equipment common to all the members of the human species, and he accounted for agreement concerning ethical judgments through the coincidence of such judgments with the conclusions of experimental reason in calculating the social utility of moral acts. In the case of religious judgments, however, there seems to be no conveniently calculable parallel against which conflicting religious claims can be tested. It follows, therefore, that concerning religious doctrines there can be no fruitful disputation; every man must consult his individual religious consciousness, the faculty of faith.

Of course, neither Hume's agnostic conclusion regarding the inapplicability of four faculties to the religious hypothesis nor his gnostic alternative based on the faculty of faith has escaped the notice of his commentators. But while they notice it, they also dismiss it as a prudential device and hence as insincere:

> When Hume was writing his *Dialogues*, freedom of discussion in Britain was complete, subject only to certain agreed limitations—that there be no advocacy of atheism and no direct challenge to the supreme claims of the Christian faith. . . . In this outward deference to current beliefs and practices Hume was conscious of taking the ancients, especially Cicero, as his model; and it was a game into which he could zestfully enter.[6]

B. A. O. Williams agrees that Hume employed a common contrivance to escape censure as an atheist:

> One such method was to claim that one was criticising not Christianity, but superstitious perversions of it; another was

6. Kemp Smith, in Hume's *Dialogues*, pp. 39 f.

to claim that in destroying pretensions to rational argument in support of religious doctrines, one was only making way for Faith, on which they should properly rest.

Williams remarks that Kant also claimed to be removing Reason to make way for Faith. But, Williams continues:

> The difference is that he meant it, and Hume and Bayle did not.[7]

This view, while it is compatible with the evidence, relies largely on a motivational interpretation which, I believe, misconstrues Hume's character and distorts his philosophy. The opposing view, which takes serious cognizance of Hume's assertions concerning the capacity of faith to apprehend some positive elements of a religious hypothesis, is not based on a naïvely literal acceptance of Hume's ostensible doctrines, although its main evidence is textual. It is a view that coheres as well, if not better, than its opposite with the undisputed elements of his faculty theory of knowledge.[8] It is also one that agrees with Jessop's estimation that "we are unlikely to reach a just understanding of either the man or his work unless we take into account his judgment upon himself."[9] If we do this, we find that Hume certainly did not consider himself to be an atheist. He denied that appellation where it would have been easiest for him to have acknowledged it—namely, in the company of the militant French *Philosophes*, whose views he is alleged to have

---

7. In *David Hume, a Symposium*, ed. D. F. Pears (London: Macmillan, 1963).
8. This view is suggested in C. W. Hendel, *Studies in the Philosophy of David Hume* (Princeton: Princeton University Press, 1925), p. 285; T. E. Jessop, "Some Misunderstandings of Hume," *Revue Internationale de Philosophie* 6 (1952): 157; R. Sternfeld, "The Unity of Hume's *Enquiry concerning Human Understanding*," *Review of Metaphysics* 3, no. 2 (undated reprint): 179.
9. Jessop, p. 157.

shared.[10] But if Hume did maintain the validity of cognitions of faith as a genuine rather than as a prudential philosophical doctrine, it is clear that the cognitions of faith to which he assented differed radically from the Church dogmas of his time. Thus, even though it is unjust to consider him an atheist in the philosophical sense, his contemporaries were probably right in considering him an infidel in the ecclesiastical sense. Hume's was a mitigated faith which excluded much and admitted little. Its nature and limits are perhaps best summed up in a passage from a letter in which he comments on a sermon dealing with the efficacy of prayer:

> I have read Mr. Leechman's Sermon with a great deal of pleasure and think it a very good one; though I am sorry to find the author to be a rank atheist. You know (or ought to know) that Plato says there are three kinds of atheists. The first who deny a deity, the second who deny his providence, the third who assert that he is influenced by prayers or sacrifices. I find Mr. Leechman is an atheist of the last kind. . . . As to the argument, I could wish Mr. Leechman would in the second edition answer this objection both to devotion and prayer, and indeed to everything we commonly call religion, except the practice of morality and the assent of the understanding [not of reason] to the proposition that God exists.[11]

In proposing that faith is an independent faculty for the apprehension of the irrational concepts of religion, Hume's theory accords with those of theologians who assert the primacy of faith over reason in that particular sphere. And it also agrees with the doctrines of philosophers who, while wishing to maintain as true some elements of the religious hypothesis, have abandoned as

---

10. E. C. Mossner, *The Life of David Hume* (Edinburgh: Nelson, 1954), p. 483.
11. D. Hume, *New Letters of David Hume*, ed. Klibansky and Mossner (Oxford: Oxford University Press, 1954), pp. 10 ff.

impossible the task of providing such elements with intellectual proofs. So much is granted, be it ever so reluctantly and circuitously, even by Hume's most vehement opponents. A striking instance of this is provided by A. E. Taylor who, after describing Hume's remarks on the insufficiency of reason and the need for faith as "a mere piece of mockery," restates what is, in effect, Hume's position:

> It would involve an obvious circle in our reasoning if we alleged the occurrence of miraculous events as the ground for adopting a theistic metaphysic . . . . And I think it follows that we cannot expect to arrive at a metaphysic of any great worth so long as we confine our contemplation to the domain of formal logic, or epistemology, or even of experimental science.[12]

The same position is restated elsewhere by Taylor:

> It would certainly be the grossest presumption to maintain that the Absolute can contain no higher types of finite individuality than those presented by human society; on the other hand, it would be equally presumptuous to assert that we have reasoned knowledge of their existence and their direct social relation with ourselves. Hence we must, I think, be content to say that the hypothesis, so far as it seems to be suggested to any one of us by the concrete facts of his own individual experience, is a matter for the legitimate exercise of Faith.[13]

It is possible to take Hume's doctrine as going even beyond this point. In establishing a sharp epistemological

---

12. A. E. Taylor, *Philosophical Studies* (London: Macmillan, 1934), p. 363.

13. A. E. Taylor, *Elements of Metaphysics* (London: Methuen, 1961), 400. Unless we take the position that Taylor meant it while Hume and Bayle did not (see reference to B. A. O. Williams above), this seems to be an admirable restatement of Hume's rational agnosticism coupled with the doctrine of religious cognition by faith. (*Cf. Enquiry*, pp. 127, 129 ff.)

demarcation between religious and nonreligious cognitions, Hume has anticipated in eighteenth-century terms
the kind of distinction that Wittgenstein has drawn in
twentieth-century terms. Wittgenstein's thesis can be
summed up as maintaining that, while religious and nonreligious (especially empirical) locutions share the same
vocabulary—*belief, historicity, evidence, reasons, grounds,*
and so on—this vocabulary takes on entirely different
shades of meaning when it is employed in religious and
in nonreligious contexts.

To take only one instance: in empirical discourse, the
term *believe* (as in "I believe that Joe is married") suggests a reckoning with direct observational evidence or
documentary evidence or reliable reports. In the absence
of any such evidence, the assertion of belief would be
irrelevant or meaningless. But such is not the case in respect of assertions concerning religious beliefs:

> Whatever believing in God may be, it can't be believing in
> something we can test, or find means of testing. . . . The mere
> fact that someone says they believe on evidence doesn't tell
> me enough for me to be able to say now whether I can say
> of a sentence "God exists" that your evidence is unsatisfactory
> or insufficient.[14]

The same appreciation by Hume of the applicative dis-
parity between the religious and the nonreligious uses of
"believe" is to be found in Boswell's account of his inter-
view with the dying philosopher:

> But I maintained my Faith. I told him that I believed the
> Christian Religion as I believed History. Said [Hume]: "You
> do not believe it as you believe the Revolution."[15]

14. L. Wittgenstein, *Lectures and Conversations on Aesthetics, Psychology and Religious Belief*; ed. C. Barrett (Oxford: Basil Blackwell,
1966) , p. 60.
15. *Dialogues*, p. 77.

Again, neither for Hume (as here interpreted) nor for Wittgenstein does the denial of a theological assertion entail its contradictory. It is not a matter of "yes" or "no," of theism or atheism. Rather, it is for Hume a matter of the employment of different faculties, and for Wittgenstein a matter of different planes of meaning:

> Religion is founded on *Faith*, not on reason; and it is a sure method of exposing it to put it to such a trial as it is, by no means, fitted to endure.[16]

> Suppose that someone believed in the Last Judgement, and I don't, does this mean that I believe the opposite to him, just that there won't be such a thing? I would say: "not at all, or not always" . . .
> If some said: "Wittgenstein, do you believe in this?" I'd say: "No." "Do you contradict the man?" I'd say: "No". . . .
> It isn't a question of my being anywhere near him, but on an entirely different plane, which you could express by saying: "You mean something altogether different, Wittgenstein."[17]

Theology and Matters of Fact

Hume's method of investigating the relation of faith to cognitive spheres other than religion does not consist, as in the case of his treatment of the other faculties, of an analysis of what we can believe on faith in these cognitive spheres. Rather, his investigation turns on what we can infer regarding these spheres, once we have assented by faith to the proposition that God exists.

In relation to matters of fact, the question that Hume examines is whether we can account for specific instances

---

16. *Enquiry*, p. 130.
17. Wittgenstein, *Lectures and Conversations*, p. 53.

of causal conjunctions in terms of immediate volitions of God:

> Instead of saying that one billiard-ball moves another by a force which it has derived from the author of nature, it is the Deity himself, they say, who, by a particular volition, moves the second ball, being determined to this operation by the impulse of the first ball, in consequence of those general laws which he has laid down to himself in the government of the universe.[18]

That this postulate is itself not supported by experimental reasoning has already been argued. The question now is whether, assuming the postulate, it can provide experimental reason with a better basis for its calculations than that provided by Hume's descriptive account of the causal calculus. To this, Hume proposes a negative answer. It is to the effect that, if we are unable by the use of our faculties to observe the actual causal operation of one present body on another present body, we are certainly in no better position to exercise our faculties in observing the operation of "a mind, even the supreme mind" either on itself or on body:

> We surely comprehend as little the operations of one as of the other. Is it more difficult to conceive that motion may arise from impulse than that it may arise from volition? All we know is our profound ignorance in both cases.[19]

But even if the divine volition explanation is the correct one, it will be of no use in increasing our predictive accuracy. Either we shall have to concede that God's inscrutability makes all predictions uncertain; or, if we claim that God's volitions operate with discernible regu-

---

18. *Enquiry*, p. 70.
19. *Ibid.*, pp. 72 f.

larity, then we shall need to calculate the probability of future conjunctions between causes and effects from the observed frequency with which God has willed these causes and effects to be conjoined in the past.

A religious solution to the problem of induction fails to solve or to dissolve the problem: it merely shifts our attention from the observational investigation of conjunctions among events to the investigation by the same means of conjunctions between divine volition and events. Hume's argument tends not so much to exclude the possibility of the religious solution as to call into question its usefulness either for predictive purposes or as an explanation of causal conjunctions. And since there seem to be no independent arguments in its favor, this particular solution is discarded.

Theology and Percepts

Analogous tactics may be employed in discounting the relevance of God's existence and his supposed attributes to the question of whether "the perceptions of the senses be produced by external objects, resembling them."[20] Starting from the position that there is a duality of percepts and objects to which these percepts relate, our acceptance of the postulate that it is God who assures the coincidence of these two types of entity does not provide us with any more information as to the mechanism by which it is achieved than does any other theory claiming to explain the coincidence. And again, even if it is granted that God effects the coincidence, and even if we understood the mechanism whereby he does this, such knowl-

----

20. *Ibid.*, p. 153.

edge would not enhance our acquaintance with these external bodies; for (by the terms of the dualistic theory) we would still be limited to what is apprehended in perception. Neither would it enhance our ability to infer any relationship thought to exist among percepts or between percepts and objects. Such inferences would still have to depend on the experimental calculus of what these relations have been found in experience to be, or on the experimental calculus of what God has been observed to make these relations be.

Hume's argument on this topic relies on two other considerations. The first of these is the claim that the question of the relationship of percepts to external objects is a question of fact; and, as such, the only just means of determining the nature of the relationship is by the calculus of experimental reasoning. This implicitly excludes any hypothesis based on the supposed regulation of percepts with objects by divine intervention, since we are excluded (in Hume's theory) from observing any such regulatory process by reason of the fact that our sensory apprehensions are limited to the apprehension of impressions.[21] The second consideration relates to the absurd consequences which, Hume claims, follow from "recourse to the veracity of the supreme Being, in order to prove the veracity of our senses":

> If his veracity were at all concerned in this matter, our senses would be entirely infallible; because it is not possible that he can ever deceive. Not to mention, that, if the external world be once called in question, we shall be at a loss to find arguments, by which we may prove the existence of that Being or any of his attributes.[22]

21. *Ibid.*
22. *Ibid.*

Against the first, it might be urged that if Hume's doctrine implicitly excludes the possibility of our being aware of divine regulation, then it is the doctrine that is wrong rather than the excluded hypothesis. His second argument seems to contain more serious weaknesses. It is by no means clear, for example, that the absurd consequences which he claims to draw from the proposition are in fact entailed by it. But even if his deduction is correct, it might be held, as indeed Hume himself suggests in another connection,[23] that this (unlike the *truth* of its consequences) has no relevance to the validity of an argument. Hume can, however, rely on a second line of defense against the divine regulation of percepts with objects: namely, his arguments against hypothesizing the dualism of percepts and objects in any form. If we can have no knowledge of objects in the first instance, then presumably there is no point in attempting to explain how such unknown objects relate to percepts. Ultimately, therefore, the validity of his objections to the religious explanation depends on the strength—or weakness—of his theory of perception.

Theology and Value Judgments

In considering the relation of God's existence to the sphere of ethics, Hume limits himself to a discussion of the ethical consequences of the doctrine of divine predestination.[24] His argument is the popular but unrigorous one that, if all human actions are preordained by God, then either such actions "can have no moral turpitude at all" or "they must involve our Creator in the same guilt." Hume examines some of the possible escapes from this

---

23. *Ibid.*, p. 96.
24. *Ibid.*, pp. 99 ff.

apparent dilemma: for example, the theory that individual ills really serve to enhance a beneficent whole. What he asserts to be the flaws in such devices, together with the absurdity and impiety of the conclusions entailed by the doctrine of predestination, lead him to deduce that the doctrine itself "cannot possibly be true." Logically, of course, the doctrine can be true: we may accept either of the impious consequences; or we may find on closer examination that the doctrine entails a quite different and acceptable consequence; or the terms *good* and *evil* in their ethical sense are properly applicable to predestined actions; or these terms are applicable to actions that are predestined but that we do not know to be predestined. However, taking into account the limited number of factors with which Hume operates, and the interpretation that he puts on them, it is correct to say that the doctrine of predestination is incompatible, not with God's existence, but with the concept of a perfectly good God or, if the perfect goodness of God is retained, with the existence of evil in the world.

Whether God's existence is relevant to ethics is not bound up exclusively with the doctrine of predestination; and it is not a question that is automatically decided in the negative by the simple expedient of discrediting that doctrine. However, Hume's theory of experimental reason can be said to imply a tentatively negative answer to the problem, even if we disregard the dubious doctrine of predestination and its dubious refutation. From God's existence alone, nothing can be inferred except what (if anything) is entailed by "existence." Consequently, in order for God to become relevant to ethics, we require independent knowledge of one or more additional premises: that God desires moral conduct from mankind, or that the Bible constitutes God's moral legislation for the world. Both these premises incorporate matters of fact; and their validity is therefore to be weighed by the standards of experimental reason. But experimental reason supports neither, for nothing can be inductively inferred about God's attributes or his governance of the world except what we can observe in the world, and this is hardly such as to warrant belief in an overall beneficent governor.[25]

Nevertheless, it is still consistent with Hume's doctrines for us to accept either or both additional premises on faith, in the same way that it is possible to take the primary premise—God's existence—on faith. But if this is so, it follows from the character of the cognitions of faith that ethical disputes will take the form of mutually contradictory and mutually incontestable assertions regarding what A's God desires or what A's sacred scriptures enjoin as opposed to what B's God desires or what B's sacred scriptures enjoin. And the solution by faith will leave unresolved the question of whether an action is morally good because it is divinely prescribed, or whether it is divinely prescribed because it is morally good. If the former is the case, then the question arises whether a previously "good" action can become morally reprehensible merely as a consequence of a change in the divine prescription; and if the latter is the case, then the religious solution merely transfers the problem from a question of what it is that constitutes the good for man to a question of what it is that constitutes the good for God. Hence, while it is conceivable that faith and theology do have some bearing on moral behavior, neither seems to go very far in solving any of the fundamental problems involved in the cognition of evaluative judgments.

---

25. *Ibid.*, pp. 137, 141–42.

9

Conclusion

The primary object of the foregoing exposition has been to present Hume's first *Enquiry* as a systematic account of his mental geography or faculty theory of knowledge. Although this is what the *Enquiry* claims to be, Hume's many commentators have generally not recognized it as such and have tended to treat it as a collection of essays on various topics.

At first sight, the *Enquiry* does in fact appear to consist of dissertations on separate epistemological, religious, and other topics. The difficulty of sorting out these elements into a clearly defined faculty theory of knowledge is owing in large measure to the method adopted by Hume in presenting the theory. His approach was to select an individual cognitive sphere or a characteristic problem in an individual cognitive sphere and to train on it in turn each of the mental faculties. By this technique he investigated what information, if any, can be derived in that sphere by the exercise of the various cognitive faculties. The conclusions arising from this series of investigations contain all the elements of the faculty theory of knowledge; but the elements lie scattered among disparate discussions on the origin of our knowledge of causes, the credibility of evidence for miracles, relations of ideas, and other isolated problems.

The premise underlying the present work has been that a clearer topographical view of the mental geography can be obtained by retaining the elements of Hume's theory but reversing his expository procedure. Thus, we have taken each mental faculty in turn and applied it systematically to the varieties of cognitive spheres or to characteristic problems within such spheres.

By either method of exposition we find the conclusions of Hume's argument to be as follows: that abstract reason can elicit knowledge in the field of relations of ideas, but that it is inapplicable to matters of fact, value judgments, and theology; that experimental reason is appropriate for the estimation of probabilities in the field of matters of fact, but that its calculations are at best inconclusive when they are concerned with percepts, value judgments, and theology; that perception is the proper means of identifying our impressions and ideas, but that its powers do not extend into the sphere of relations of ideas, value judgments, or theology; that mental taste determines the nature of value judgments, but that these judgments cannot then be applied to the field of theology; and that faith is the proper foundation for theological beliefs, but that these beliefs have no bearing on matters of fact, percepts, or value judgments. This sums up the faculty theory of knowledge.

Since there is only one cognitive sphere to which any

given faculty can be properly applied, while there are several to which it can not, any complete faculty theory of knowledge such as Hume's will tend, for simple arithmetic reasons, to be predominantly concerned with negative rather than with positive epistemological conclusions. This tendency is reinforced in Hume's work because he was concerned with more than the straightforward exposition of the theory. He was concerned also with discrediting the then-prevalent practice of founding all knowledge on a single epistemological or methodological principle.

Hume's preoccupation with the negative aspects of the faculty theory of knowledge has led to its being construed as advocating some form of scepticism or epistemological agnosticism. Such an interpretation ignores Hume's doctrines concerning the possibility of positive knowledge in the major fields of human intellectual endeavor—even if that knowledge is limited, and even if in many instances it is irrational. The attribution to Hume of variously defined species of scepticism, atheism, phenomenalism, and other extreme doctrines results from inattention to the overall theory, the mental geography, which contains gnostic as well as agnostic epistemological conclusions.

We have seen that the *Enquiry* claims to be the elaboration of a faculty theory of knowledge and that its disparate elements fit naturally into the framework of such a theory. Viewing the *Enquiry* in this light not only makes that work itself more comprehensible but it provides the basis for a new and more coherent conception of the relationship of the *Enquiry* to Hume's other major works.

The *Treatise* may be viewed, in accordance with this interpretation and with its stated aim, as the detailed development of one particular aspect of the mental geography: namely, the extent to which knowledge is attainable in various cognitive fields through the application of experimental reason. Since experimental reason has only a limited application, and since the *Treatise* deals with a range of topics many of which lie outside of these limits, it is not surprising to find that the *Treatise* has a predominantly sceptical tendency and, consequently, that those commentators who take the *Treatise* as the primary text for the exegesis of Hume conclude that Hume's philosophy is "sheerly negative."

Similarly, the *Dialogues* may be viewed as a detailed examination of another fragment of the mental geography: namely, the conclusions for theology of submitting the religious hypothesis to the test of experimental and, to a lesser extent, of abstract reasoning. And again, since it forms part of Hume's theory that this is to submit the hypothesis to a test which it is by no means fitted to endure, it is not surprising to find the *Dialogues* containing conclusions that are unfavorable to the hypothesis, or to find that these conclusions are taken to reflect Hume's final, sheerly negative, position on that subject.

Similarly, too, the *Enquiry concerning the Principles of Morals* may be viewed as developing yet another aspect of the same theory: this time, the results of the correct application of the moral sentiment to ethical cognitions and an examination of the supplementary and confirmatory role played in this field by experimental reason applied to the concomitant matters of fact. Here too, perhaps, it is not surprising to find, since Hume was at last presenting a predominantly positive doctrine, that he could describe this work (in his autobiographical essay) as "incomparably the best" of all his writings. Perhaps for the same reason, the second *Enquiry* is preeminent in the estimation of his critics, while the first *Enquiry*— which presents in full that theory of which his other works are partial elaborations—languishes in relative neglect.

Bibliography

Adrian, E. D. *The Physical Background of Perception.*
Oxford: Oxford University Press, 1947.

Armstrong, D. M. *Perception and the Physical World.*
London: Routledge and Kegan Paul, 1961.

Atkinson, R. F. "Hume on Mathematics," *Philosophical
Quarterly* 10 (1960).

Ayer, A. J. *The Foundations of Empirical Knowledge.*
London: Macmillan, 1963.

———. *Language Truth and Logic.* 2nd ed. London:
Gollancz, 1964.

———. "Phenomenalism," *Proceedings of the Aristotelian
Society.* 47 (1946-47).

Basson, A. H. *David Hume.* Harmondsworth: Penguin,
1958.

Belgion, M. *David Hume.* London: Longmans, Green &
Co., 1965.

Bennett, J. "Analytic-Synthetic," *Proceedings of the Aristotelian Society.* 59 (1958-59).

Bohr, N. "On the Notions of Causality and Complementarity," *Dialectica* 2 (1948).

Britton, K.; Urmson, J. O.; Kneale, W. Symposium: "Are

143

Necessary Truths True by Convention?" *Proceedings of the Aristotelian Society,* supp. vol. 21 (1947).

Broad, C. D. *Five Types of Ethical Theory.* London: Routledge and Kegan Paul, 1930.

———. "Some Elementary Reflexions on Sense-Perception," *Philosophy* 27 (1952).

Burtt, E. A. *Types of Religious Philosophy.* New York: Harper, 1939.

Butler, R. J. "Hume's Perception." Papers presented at seminars at the Institute of Advanced Studies, Australian National University, 1963.

Cassirer, E. *The Problem of Knowledge.* Translated by Woglom and Hendel. New Haven: Yale University Press, 1950.

Chisholm, R. M. *Perceiving: A Philosophical Study.* Ithaca: Cornell University Press, 1957.

Church, R. W. *Hume's Theory of the Understanding.* London: Allen and Unwin, 1935.

Creed, J. M. and Smith, J. S. B. *Religious Thought in the Eighteenth Century.* Cambridge: Cambridge University Press, 1934.

Elkin, W. B. "Relation of *The Treatise of Human Nature* (Book I) to *The Enquiry concerning Human Understanding,*" *Philosophical Review* 3 (1894).

Engels, F. *Dialectics of Nature.* 3rd ed. Moscow: Progress Publishers, 1964.

Feigl, H. "The Logical Character of the Principle of Induction," *Readings in Philosophical Analysis.* New York: Appleton-Century-Crofts, 1949.

Flew, A. *God and Philosophy.* London: Hutchinson, 1966.

———. *Hume's Philosophy of Belief.* London: Routledge and Kegan Paul, 1961.

———. "On the Interpretation of Hume," *Philosophy* 38 (1963).

Furlong, E. J. "Imagination in Hume's *Treatise* and *Enquiry concerning the Human Understanding*," *Philosophy* 36 (1961).

Good, I. J. *The Estimation of Probabilities: An Essay in Modern Bayesian Methods.* Cambridge, Mass.: M.I.T. Press, 1965.

―――. *Probability and the Weighing of Evidence.* London: Griffin, 1950.

Greig, J. Y. T. *David Hume.* London: Jonathan Cape, 1931.

Grice, H. P. and Strawson, P. F. "In Defense of a Dogma," *Classics of Analytical Philosophy.* Edited by R. R. Ammerman. New York: McGraw-Hill, 1965.

Gross, M. W. "Whitehead's Answer to Hume," *Journal of Philosophy* 38 (1941).

Hartshorne, C. "Hume's Metaphysics and Its Present-Day Influence," *New Scholasticism* 25 (1961).

Haymond, W. F. "Hume's Phenomenalism," *Modern Schoolman* 41 (1963-64).

Hendel, C. W. *Studies in the Philosophy of David Hume.* Princeton: Princeton University Press, 1925.

Hobart, R. E. "Hume without Scepticism," *Mind* 39 (1930).

Hume, D. *An Abstract of A Treatise of Human Nature.* Reprinted with an Introduction by Keynes and Sraffa. Cambridge: Cambridge University Press, 1938.

―――. *Dialogues concerning Natural Religion.* Edited by N. K. Smith. 2nd ed. with supplement. Edinburgh: Nelson, 1947.

―――. *Enquiries concerning the Human Understanding and concerning the Principles of Morals.* Edited by L. A. Selby-Bigge. 2nd ed. Oxford: Oxford University Press, 1902.

―――. *The Letters of David Hume.* (2 vols.; edited by

146   A FACULTY THEORY OF KNOWLEDGE

J. Y. T. Greig) Oxford: Oxford University Press, 1932.

———. *New Letters of David Hume.* Edited by R. Klibansky and E. C. Mossner. Oxford: Oxford University Press, 1954.

———. *A Treatise of Human Nature.* (2 vols.) London: Dent, 1911.

Huxley, T. *Hume.* London: Macmillan, 1909.

Jeffreys, H. *Theory of Probability.* (3rd ed.) Oxford: Oxford University Press, 1961.

Jessop, T. E. "Some Misunderstandings of Hume," *Revue Internationale de Philosophie* 6 (1951).

Kant, I. *Critique of Practical Reason and Other Works on the Theory of Ethics.* Translated by T. K. Abbott. 6th ed. London: Longmans, 1909.

Keene, J. B. "Analytical Statements and Mathematical Truth," *Analysis* 15 (1954-55).

Kruse, V. *Hume's Philosophy in His Principal Work: A Treatise of Human Nature and in His Essays.* Translated by P. T. Federspiel. London: Oxford University Press, 1939.

Kydd, R. M. *Reason and Conduct in Hume's Treatise.* London: Oxford University Press, 1946.

Laing, B. M. *David Hume.* London: Ernest Benn, 1932.

Laird, J. *Hume's Philosophy of Human Nature.* London: Methuen, 1932.

Lillie, W. *An Introduction to Ethics.* London: Methuen, 1955.

Mace, C. A. "Hume's Doctrine of Causality," *Proceedings of the Aristotelian Society* 32 (1931-32).

MacNabb, D. G. C. "David Hume," *Encyclopedia of Philosophy* 4. Edited by Paul Edwards. New York: Macmillan and Free Press, 1967.

———. *David Hume: His Theory of Knowledge and Morality*. London: Hutchinson, 1951.

———. "Hume on Induction," *Revue Internationale de Philosophie* 6 (1952).

Marx, K. and Engels, F. *On Religion*. Moscow: Foreign Languages Publishing House, 1955.

Mascall, E. L. "Perception and Sensation," *Proceedings of the Aristotelian Society* 64 (1963-64).

Maund, C. *Hume's Theory of Knowledge*. London: Macmillan, 1937.

———. "On the Nature and Significance of Hume's Scepticism," *Revue Internationale de Philosophie* 6 (1952).

Miller, D. S. "Hume's Deathblow to Deductivism," *Journal of Philosophy* 46 (1949).

———. "Professor Donald Williams versus Hume," *Journal of Philosophy* 44 (1947).

Moore, G. E. *Philosophical Studies*. London: Routledge and Kegan Paul, 1922.

———. "The Refutation of Idealism," *Mind* 12 (1903).

———. *Some Main Problems of Philosophy*. London: Allen and Unwin, 1953.

Morris, C. R. *Locke Berkeley Hume*. Oxford: Oxford University Press, 1931.

Mossner, E. C. "The Continental Reception of Hume's *Treatise*, 1739-1741," *Mind* 56 (1947).

———. "The First Answer to Hume's *Treatise:* An Unnoticed Item of 1740," *Journal of the History of Ideas* 12 (1951).

———. *The Life of David Hume*. Edinburgh: Nelson, 1954.

Oppenheimer, J. R. *The Flying Trapeze: Three Crises for Physicists*. London: Oxford University Press, 1964.

Passmore, J. A. *Hume's Intentions.* Cambridge: Cambridge University Press, 1952.

Pears, D. F., ed. *David Hume, a Symposium.* London: Macmillan, 1963.

Penfield, W. *The Excitable Cortex in Conscious Man.* Liverpool: Liverpool University Press, 1958.

Pieron, H. *The Sensations: Their Functions, Processes, and Mechanisms.* Translated by Pirenne and Abbott. London: Frederick Muller, 1952.

Price, H. H. *Hume's Theory of the External World.* Oxford: Oxford University Press, 1940.

————. "The Permanent Significance of Hume's Philosophy," *Philosophy* 15 (1940).

Prichard, H. A. *Knowledge and Perception.* Oxford: Oxford University Press, 1950.

Putnam, H. "The Analytic and the Synthetic," *Minnesota Studies in the Philosophy of Science* 3. Edited by H. Feigl and G. Maxwell. Minneapolis: University of Minnesota Press, 1962.

Quine, W. V. O. *From a Logical Point of View.* Cambridge, Mass.: Harvard University Press, 1953.

————. *Word and Object.* Cambridge, Mass.: M.I.T. Press, 1960.

Quinton, A. M. "The Problem of Perception," *Mind* 64 (1955).

Reichenbach, H. "A Conversation between Bertrand Russell and David Hume," *Journal of Philosophy* 46 (1949).

————. "On the Justification of Induction," *Readings in Philosophical Analysis.* Edited by Feigl and Sellars. New York: Appleton-Century-Crofts, 1949.

Reid, T. *Essays on the Intellectual Powers of Man.* Edited by A. D. Woozley. London: Macmillan, 1941.

Robson, J. W. "Whitehead's Answer to Hume," *Journal of Philosophy* 38 (1941).

Russell, B. *Human Knowledge.* New York: Simon and Schuster, 1948.

————. "Knowledge by Acquaintance and Knowledge by Description," *Proceedings of the Aristotelian Society* 11 (1910-11).

————. *An Outline of Philosophy.* London: Allen and Unwin, 1932.

Ryle, G. *The Concept of Mind.* Harmondsworth: Penguin, 1963.

Santayana, G. *Scepticism and Animal Faith.* London: Constable, 1923.

Schiller, F. C. S. "Humism and Humanism," *Proceedings of the Aristotelian Society* 7 (1906-7).

Scriven, M. *Primary Philosophy.* New York: McGraw-Hill, 1966.

Seth, A. *Scottish Philosophy: A Comparison of the Scottish and German Answers to Hume.* Edinburgh: Blackwood, 1885.

Smith, J. W. "Concerning Hume's Intentions," *Philosophical Revue* 69 (1960).

Smith, N. K. "David Hume: 1739-1939," *Proceedings of the Aristotelian Society,* sup. vol. 18 (1939).

————. "The Naturalism of Hume," *Mind* 14 (1905).

————. *The Philosophy of David Hume.* London: Macmillan, 1964.

Stace, W. T. "The Refutation of Realism," in *A Modern Introduction to Philosophy.* Edited by Edwards and Pap. New York: Free Press of Glencoe, 1962.

Sternfeld, R. *"The Unity of Hume's Enquiry concerning Human Understanding," Review of Metaphysics* 3, no. 2 (undated reprint).

Strawson, P. F. *Introduction to Logical Theory.* London: Methuen, 1952.

Taylor, A. E. *Philosophical Studies.* London: Macmillan, 1934.

———. *Elements of Metaphysics.* London: Methuen, 1961.

Taylor, H. "Hume's Answer to Whitehead," *Journal of Philosophy* 38 (1941).

Underhill, E. *Mysticism.* London: Methuen, 1960.

Urmson, J. O. *Philosophical Analysis.* Oxford: Oxford University Press, 1956.

Whitehead, A. N. *Science and the Modern World.* New York: New American Library, 1948.

Williams, D. *The Ground of Induction.* Cambridge, Mass.: Harvard University Press, 1947.

———. "Induction and the Future," *Mind* 57 (1948).

Wittgenstein, L. *Lectures and Conversations on Aesthetics, Psychology and Religious Belief.* Edited by C. Barrett. Oxford: Blackwell, 1966.

———. *Tractatus Logico-Philosophicus.* Translated by Pears and McGuinness. London: Routledge and Kegan Paul, 1961.

Wolff, R. P. "Hume on Mental Activity," *Philosophical Review* 69 (1960).

Yolton, J. W. "A Defence of Sense-Data," *Mind* 57 (1948).

Zabeeh, F. *Hume: Precursor of Modern Empiricism.* The Hague: Martinus Nijhoff, 1960.

Index

Abstract reason, 34–35, 37, 48–50, 70, 74, 99, 109, 123; critique of Hume's theory of, 53–65; and ethics, 67; and the irrational, 66; limits of, 42; and mathematics, 38; and matters of fact, 51–53, 69, 138; and relations of ideas, 48–51, 69, 138; and religious hypothesis, 69, 140; and tautologies, 38; and theology, 67–69, 138; and value judgments, 66–67, 69, 115, 138

Abstract of a Treatise of Human Nature, 25, 27, 41; on ideas, 107; on percepts, 106

Analogy, argument from, 72–73, 79, 90–93

Analytic, 36, 41, 48–50, 52, 54–55

A posteriori, 36

A priori, 35, 48–50, 53, 58, 68

Armstrong, D. M.: on Hume, 15 n; on material objects, 89 n

Ayer, A. J.: on Hume, 56 n; on propositions, 51 n

Basson, A. H., on Hume, 15 n, 20 n, 39 n, 105 n

Bayes, T., on probability, 65

Bayle, Pierre, 126

Belief: Hume on, 75–76, 78, 84, 129; Wittgenstein on, 129–30

Bennet, J., on analyticity, 55 n

Bohr, Niels, on causality, 61

Bolzano, Bernhard, on probability, 63

Boswell, James, and Hume, 129

Broad, C. D.: on Hume, 116; on material objects, 89 n

Burtt, E. A., on miracles, 94 n

Butler, Joseph, and Hume, 22

Calculus: infinitesimal, 48–49; rational, 33, 37, 82–84, 87, 97, 110, 117, 120, 133

Campbell, George, and Hume, 22

Causality, 36, 38, 59–61, 65, 74, 78–80, 82, 85, 138; Bohr on, 61; Cartesian, 80; Engels on, 57–58; and ethics, 114; and God, 131–32; and human behavior, 73–75; Hume on, 61, 71–72, 75–78, 80–81; and matters of fact, 52–53; and perception, 89, 107; and Reid, 58; and theology, 68, 92

Chisholm, R. M.: on Hume, 14 n; on language, 56 n

151

152   A FACULTY THEORY OF KNOWLEDGE

Church, R. W., on Hume, 14 n, 56 n
Cognition, 39, 46–47, 53, 69, 89, 124–26, 128 n, 129, 136–38, 140. *See also* Knowledge
Complete enumeration, 95
Contingency, 119–20
Contradiction, law of, 50, 52–53
Cosmology, 58–60
Creed, J. M., and Smith, J. S. B., on miracles, 94 n
Criticism. *See* Value judgments

Deduction, 39, 41, 95
Deductivism, 13, 52, 66
Descartes, René, philosophy of, 13, 59, 80
Dialectical materialism, 57
Dialogues concerning Natural Religion: and faculty theory of knowledge, 140; on theology, 93, 122, 129
Divinity. *See* Theology
Dualism, 100, 132–34

Empirical proof, 95–98
Engels, Friedrich, on induction, 57–58
Enquiry concerning the Human Understanding, 11; on abstract reason, 48–53, 55, 62, 66–69; aim of, 29–32; on experimental reason, 71–80, 82, 84–85, 87–89, 91–98; and faculty theory of knowledge, 33–39, 46, 137, 139–41; on faith, 124, 130–34, 136; Hume's epistemology in, 13–14, 16–17; on perception, 100–103, 105, 107–11; relation of, to *Treatise of Human Nature,* 18–28, 40–45, 139–40; N. K. Smith on, 122; on taste, 114–15, 117–19
Enquiry concerning the Principles of Morals, 18; on ethics, 66; and faculty theory of knowledge, 140–41
Epistemology, 47, 56, 139; eighteenth century, 12; in *Enquiry*

concerning the Human Understanding, 94–95; of Hume, 13–17, 35, 47, 80, 106, 122; of logical positivists, 36; of rationalists, 35; and religion, 67–68; of Wittgenstein, 36
Ethics, 36, 67, 86–87, 99, 114–18, 125, 138; and God, 120–21, 134–36; and religious hypothesis, 118, 123–24. *See also* Value judgments
Existence, 34, 38, 51–53, 70, 89, 124, 135
Experience, 36, 72–73, 89, 111–13, 120, 123
Experimental reason, 34–37, 48, 70–98, 99, 109–10, 123–25, 131, 135–36, 140; and causality, 38; and existence, 38, 89; limits of, 42–43; and matters of fact, 38, 70–86, 138; and percepts, 87–90, 138; and theology, 68, 90–98, 138, 140; and value judgments, 67, 86–87, 116, 138, 140
Euthyphro fallacy, 86

Faculties, 14, 31–32, 37, 39, 46–47, 117, 122–24; irrational, 33–34, 37, 84, 124; rational, 33–34, 37, 67, 74, 83; and religion, 125, 127, 130
Faculty theory of knowledge, 13, 16, 30–39, 46–48, 66, 94, 126, 137–41. *See also* Abstract reason; Experimental reason; Faith; Knowing, ways of; Perception; Reason; Taste; Understanding
Faith, 34, 38, 122–36, 138
Feigl, H., on induction, 62–64
Flew, Antony: on faculty theory of knowledge, 16 n, 39, 41; on Hume, 14 n, 16 n, 25 n, 39 n, 56 n, 81 n; on meaning, 103–4; on perception, 105; on religion, 90 n, 111 n
Furlong, E. J., on Hume, 25 n, 105 n

Galileo, influence of, 59